THE
WEALTH
BLUEPRINT

Napoleon Hill (1883–1970), best known for his global bestseller *Think and Grow Rich*, was a self-help author and businessman whose work has influenced millions across the world, from Norman Vincent Peale to Donald Trump. Born poor, Hill lived a colourful life, pursuing several different business ventures and professions. He also met and advised many famous people, such as US President Woodrow Wilson. Hill eventually found widespread success as a motivational author, writing several books on how to achieve success and practically creating the self-help genre.

THE WEALTH BLUEPRINT

Mastering the Art of Wealth Creation

NAPOLEON HILL

RUPA

Published by
Rupa Publications India Pvt. Ltd 2024
7/16, Ansari Road, Daryaganj
New Delhi 110002

Sales centres:
Bengaluru Chennai
Hyderabad Jaipur Kathmandu
Kolkata Mumbai Prayagraj

Edition copyright © Rupa Publications India Pvt. Ltd 2024

All rights reserved.
No part of this publication may be reproduced, transmitted,
or stored in a retrieval system, in any form or by any means, electronic,
mechanical, photocopying, recording or otherwise, without the prior
permission of the publisher.

P-ISBN: 978-93-5702-742-7
E-ISBN: 978-93-5702-897-4

First impression 2024

10 9 8 7 6 5 4 3 2 1

Printed in India

This book is sold subject to the condition that it shall not, by way of
trade or otherwise, be lent, resold, hired out, or otherwise circulated,
without the publisher's prior consent, in any form of binding or
cover other than that in which it is published.

CONTENTS

1. It Is up to You to Live the Life the Creator Gave You	7
2. The Beginning of All Riches	23
3. The Attitude that Brings Wealth and Peace of Mind	33
4. Specialized Knowledge	48
5. Applied Faith	59
6. Enthusiasm	67
7. Learn to See	81
8. The Habit of Saving	96
9. The Secret of Getting Things Done	110
10. Will You Master Money? Or Will It Master You?	123
11. Growth Through Struggle	138

1

IT IS UP TO YOU TO LIVE THE LIFE THE CREATOR GAVE YOU

The Golden Rule can be applied all-out in a way that will transform our economy for the better. When people are helped to turn their ideas into the realities of business and production, everyone in the United States will have more wealth and happiness. Most of us believe in man-made gods and man-made devils. Fear has no place in a well-lived life. Put your faith, not in a Creator who bosses you but One who makes it possible for you, as a human being, to win success by your own efforts.

Wealth now can be yours. Peace of mind now can be yours at the same time, but remember, this greatest of all wealth is known only to the person who possesses it.

'HELP me find peace of mind,' the rich man said.

This was some years ago. A trip across the country was not then a matter of six hours in a jet plane, but he had come across the country to talk to me. 'I have everything money can buy,' he said, 'and I have lived long enough to find out that money cannot buy peace of mind. Please help me find it.'

A good part of this chapter consists of what we discussed, and which I shall give to you in a conversational manner. First we went into everything this book has covered—I shall omit that part—and then we branched out into what has been for many years my most cherished project.

It is a business project—and a peace-of-mind project. It could bring joy and prosperity to millions of men and women, especially to those who need help in finding their places in life. It would work hand in hand with our American economy. It would not be a 'make work' project, since it would provide services whose need is proved. It would make profit—that indispensable factor whose virtues have at length been recognized even in the Soviet Union. It would be a business project that first of all would be a human project devoted to creating wealth through sharing wealth.

A job for a dedicated man. 'Before I tell you about my project,' I said to my visitor, 'I want to make it clear that it will need a dedicated man to get it going. A man who has plenty of money, plenty of time, and plenty of executive know-how, for all these are needed to turn the idea into reality. He would have to be a man who would go to work with no thought of what he would get out of his efforts. I say he would have to have plenty of money because he might lose some of his money—and he would also have to be psychologically suited to accept this fact without losing the peace of mind the project would give him.'

'Tell me more,' said the man from California.

'Well then, what I have in mind is a nationwide organization to be called The Golden Rule Industries of America.

The visitor looked puzzled. 'Where does the Golden Rule come in?'

'Suppose you had just about enough money to live on, or even less, but you had a sound business idea you wanted to develop. What would you like someone to do unto you?'

'I surely would like someone to come along and give me capital!'

'That's what I meant. The Golden Rule Industries of America would devote itself to finding people who have sound business ideas, capitalizing those ideas and helping those people get started in their businesses. Then it would follow up with business management advice, as might be necessary. It would take care of the two major factors which make businesses fail—lack of capital and unsound management. It would fill those needs for honest people who want to get ahead but cannot fill those needs for themselves.'

My visitor looked thoughtful. 'There must be thousands of such cases.'

'I am sure there are. Let me tell you of a few I know to exist.

'There is a young woman who is clever at designing. She wants to design and manufacture women's garments for the retail trade. Golden Rule Industries could set her up in business, make sure she got started on the right foot, and watch her grow. Eventually she would give employment to hundreds of people. Bear in mind that she, and every other person whom Golden Rule Industries aids with capital and business advice, will be a person who applies the Golden Rule to others, employees in particular. Golden Rule means that too.'

'I see.'

'A mechanic has built a model of an automobile which can be manufactured and sold for one thousand dollars. It will travel fifty miles to the gallon, will carry three people—ideal for the small family—and is so simple of design that its upkeep will be very small. Golden Rule Industries could set up this man in a small shop and let him expand as his business justifies. Undoubtedly the entire automobile industry would respond with better cars at lower prices.

'A bright high school boy builds excellent model airplanes. He wants to develop his skill into a national business and employ other high school boys, after school, as his staff. Golden Rule Industries could help this youth and his friends start a business and develop it.'

'That would be a wonderful head start toward a productive life!' my visitor exclaimed.

'It certainly would. I have in mind, too, a certain poor farmer. I have sympathy with poor farmers. This man wants to introduce the growing of a certain fibre plant now being developed in Africa, which can be grown in our southern states. There is an undoubted future in this, and Golden Rule Industries could provide this man with the land, machines and employees he needs.

'A young author has written a very creditable novel based on life in the mountains of Tennessee. He has not been able to get it published, but Golden Rule Industries could take it over for him and capitalize its publication if need be.

'A young lady stenographer has invented a chair so designed that it moves back and forth with the movement of the body and adjusts itself to fit the curvature of the back. This is a great idea. It will lessen fatigue, improve work and should have a tremendous market. It would be a real pay deal for Golden Rule Industries.'

'Where do these ideas come from?' my visitor wanted to know.

'Many of them represent cases I have handled for my clients. In my endeavours to help people stand on their own feet, I became aware of the many who have good ideas and plenty of ability, and need only capital and good management advice in order to get started. Now let me tell you of a rather special area in which Golden Rule Industries could do a world of good.

'In every prison there are many well-educated men capable of conducting business and educational courses for the benefit of the other inmates. This could result in these men being ready, willing and able to lead honest, useful lives when they are freed. A group of businessmen tried out this plan in the Ohio State Penitentiary, and it worked like a charm. The International Correspondence Schools contributed more than thirty-five thousand dollars' worth of textbooks. The plan could be expanded greatly—and it is society that would profit. I have personally appropriated this idea and it is creating miracles of rehabilitation in many prisons.

'A mechanic has made a model of a prefabricated dwelling made of aluminium sections. Any able man with a couple of helpers can set up the walls and roof in a day's time and start living in the house with his family while he finishes the interior. There are similar houses on the market, but this one also can be taken down as easily as it is put up, and moved to another location, without damage to its components.'

'There's profit in that idea,' said the man from California.

'Yes, and I have a number of other ideas just as profitable. Many of them need only some way to get started despite the opposition of established interests who see only that their business world be affected, without seeing the benefit to the economy at large. Now let us digress from the business ideas themselves and look at Golden Rule Industries' general policy.

'Golden Rule Industries should be developed with the idea that it will pay a profit in itself as it goes along. I would, therefore, incorporate the idea of profit-sharing. Each enterprise would pay back to the Industries 10 per cent of its net earnings. Half of this amount would go to the Industries for the use of the capital and the business management. The other 5 per cent would be used as a payment on the original investment. When the investment was fully repaid, each enterprise would pay the Industries 5 per cent of its net earnings thereafter in return for management services and other services which might be necessary.

'You can see that this policy would create a revolving fund which could be used over and over to help more and more enterprises get started. But no enterprise would be bound forever to the Industries. After it paid back its capitalization, it could leave the Industries. We wouldn't want a monopoly. But I am quite sure that even if an enterprise left the Industries, it would continue on the Golden Rule basis of sharing the wealth it creates with its own employees, for it would be apparent by then that this is the way to make a business and its people prosper.'

My visitor had arrived in my office with a woebegone face. Now he was vibrant and looked ten years younger. 'That's great!' he exclaimed. 'And I can see that one business after another would want to come in and join hands in such an undertaking. Why, it's the best way I ever heard of to prevent strikes and other labour troubles.'

'I believe it would create harmony and peace of mind where those qualities are badly needed,' I said. 'And it would create all-important self-respect in giving people an opportunity to help themselves instead of feeding at the public trough at the expense of others. The plan would have a sweeping effect on our entire economy.

'Moreover, The Golden Rule Industries of America should operate its own radio and TV station. There would be no commercials. All the broadcasting time would be devoted to teaching people, in their own homes, all the essentials of personal achievement. People would find out at last that success is an inward matter which each of us must build within himself, rather than waiting for someone to hand him what he needs. We will have a nation that does not look for "isms" to take care of it—a nation of people who will work hard to create wealth, in the happy confidence that they will receive a good share.'

'Great heavens, man!' my visitor broke in. 'You are talking about the millennium.'

'No,' I said, 'I am presenting a practical plan to save this nation from destruction by the greedy who have not yet learned the necessity—and the virtue—of sharing riches.

'Golden Rule Industries would go beyond the transformation of industry in improving this land of ours. It would run a school for training men and women for public office—everything from dog-catcher to President. I hope this school eventually would attain such status as to make sure the voters may select public servants on the basis of their ability—instead of on their astuteness in swinging votes with the application of suitable amounts of money.'

'Amen, amen!' said my visitor.

'Along with this school of political economy there would be a citizens' committee of men and women who are capable of examining and grading all candidates for public office. The people would once again come into full possession of their government.'

'Great! But don't you think there would be a great deal of opposition to your plan—both industry-wise and government-wise? After all, you shut out a lot of nice, juicy opportunities for exploitation.'

'I'd expect opposition,' I replied. 'Opposition is a healthy circumstance. It makes one either prove the soundness of his plan or discover its weaknesses. I'd expect to make adjustments as I went along.

'There are other features I have in mind for Golden Rule Industries which might provoke even more opposition. The power of the Industries' centralized buying would be such as to cause howls from those who think only of profit. When we helped our members buy homes of their own—as I believe should be done—there'd be screams of socialism—from other interests.

'When we helped Industries' members, including their employees, with such services as may be given by physicians, dentists, attorneys, even beauticians—and made sure they received the finest service at the lowest possible fees—the screams would rise to a crescendo. In the end, however, it would be recognized that the plan represents democracy operating on the highest possible scale of efficiency. All men who wish to live and let live will welcome this plan that adds so much to living. Our strength would lie in the fact that such people vastly outnumber the people who want to dominate and exploit others.'

My visitor thought a moment. 'And this would begin with finding people who have sound business ideas, and getting them into action.'

'That is right. It would bring worthy beliefs of the human mind onto the plane of worthy achievement. The more we have in the world of this process, the better world we build.'

My visitor sat a while. At last he arose and laid some large bills on my desk.

'I want you to have this honorarium in return for the help you have given me. I am going to swing into action with a new and better philosophy of life than any I ever have known in the past. I do not know if I am the man with the money, the time, the philosophy and the business experience to initiate Golden Rule Industries. But I see now what life can be when men cooperate in the production of goods and services for each other. I see why I made money but never found peace of mind. I see what has been lacking in my life, and I feel better, Dr Hill.

Yes, sir, I feel better than I have felt in years. You have done more for me than a number of doctors have been able to do.'

My visitor never returned. Golden Rule Industries still remains a dream yet, in part, it is a dream I see coming true. Our economy grows less and less the hunting ground of the industrial pirate. It is only here and there that I see the development of co-operation, but I do see that groundswell of sharing the wealth, and it is this philosophy, based on the Golden Rule, which will keep America great; not the practice of handing out government doles to people who have done nothing to deserve them.

ABSTAIN FROM MAN-MADE INFLUENCES

Peace of mind vs. man-made gods and man-made devils. The power of firm, free belief comes with an untrammelled mind: the power to turn what the human mind believes into what the human mind achieves rarely can be found by a man who is hemmed in with fear and misdirection.

There are some exceptions. You can see men in business still making money while they harm others in making it, but this type is nowhere nearly as prevalent as it was fifty years ago.

You can see exceptions elsewhere, too. Unfortunately, the human mind is capable of believing in man-made images which it sets up as Great Truths. This belief can lead to so-called achievement on its own plane; for instance, the achievement of great societies known as religions which teach that you will fry in Hell if you do not believe certain things.

I write here for strong people—for people who realize that the most cherished beliefs nevertheless can be wrong in that they hinder the development of the human spirit. They claim to develop that spirit—but they develop it as much as a man's view of the world would be developed if he walked in a narrow alley between two high walls all his life.

Regardless of your emotions right now, surely you have been impressed by the fact that the Creator provided you with control over your own power of thought and made it impossible for any person to rob you of this privilege—unless you let him.

In my decades of research into the roots of personal achievement, I came across a book called *Catalogue of the Gods*. This book gave a brief description of each of the THIRTY THOUSAND man-made gods which men have worshiped since the beginning of civilization. Yes, THIRTY THOUSAND.

These sacred objects ranged all the way from the common angle-worm to the sun which warms our earth. They included almost every conceivable object between these two extremes, such as fish, snakes, tigers, cows, birds, rivers, oceans and the genital organs of man.

Who made these objects into gods? Man himself. Which ones were authentic gods? Ask any worshiper and he would tell you, and eventually you would have a list of thirty thousand authentic gods, one just as authentic as another.

If I undertook to describe the miseries of mankind which can be laid at the feet (if they had feet) of those thirty thousand gods, and the fears and miseries and failures they have inspired in the minds of men, I would need more than one lifetime in which to do the job properly.

Man made a great step forward in his own behalf when he began to see a Creator, not gods, and removed this Creator from any connection with earthly objects. The ancient Hebrews performed this service for man. (One of the Egyptian kings appears to have come to the same conclusion some centuries before they did, but his priests saw to it that he died young.)

Yet what have we done with this belief? My own case is

the one I know best. Until my father married the woman who saved me, the family in which I grew up was dominated by fear. It contributed to the support of an organization dedicated to maintaining that fear; it is known as the Hard Shell Baptists.

A preacher could visit our community only once a month, but on those occasions I was forced to listen to four or five hours of preachment. We were thundered at with pictures of a Hell waiting to receive us with fire and brimstone, and at times I could smell the stuff burning.

One night when I was seven or eight I dreamed I was down there chained to an iron post. My body was almost covered with a great pile of fresh brimstone. Here came Satan, swishing his tail and with an evil grin he set fire to the brimstone. I awoke screaming. One needs no formal knowledge of psychology to know this is not good for any child. But when I tried to stay away from the church that gave me dreadful nightmares, I was thrashed without mercy.

The Creator I know. One day I overheard my stepmother say to my father, 'The only real devil that exists in this or any other world is the man whose business is that of making devils.' I accepted this statement instantly and never have departed from it.

I have taken pains to put into this book the fact that my father's prayers seemed to have focused powers of healing beyond medicine, which saved my life when I had typhoid fever. That was his time of faith, not fear.

In denying that I have anything to fear, I also deny that anyone has knowledge enough to tell me anything definite about the spirit that rules the universe.

A theologian might say—although these days they are becoming wary of saying it, 'Somewhere up there is Heaven, where God dwells, and all His acceptable children go there when they leave their earthly bodies, and gather around Him.' A scientist might say, 'I have turned my telescope outward into space in all directions. I have looked into space for distances equivalent to millions of light-years, but nowhere do I see the slightest trace of anything resembling Heaven.'

The Creator whom I know is not separated from me by light-years nor by any other distance. I see evidence of His existence in every blade of grass, every flower, every tree, every creature on this earth, in the order of the stars and the plants which float out there in space, in the electrons and protons of matter, and most especially in the marvellous working principles of the human mind and the body within which it operates.

If you would rather speak of a force or a presence for a limitless intelligence rather than a Creator, it is the same. It is there. Is it affected by our worship? I doubt it. Can we sometimes attune ourselves so that we receive help from universal vibrations? This, I believe, is almost certainly true.

THE FINAL TRUTH

I do not even attempt to guess the over-all purpose or plan behind the universe. So far as I can tell, there is no plan for man except to come into this world, live a little while, and go. While he lives he is given the opportunity to make himself and his fellow men better beings, perhaps a more advanced form of man, as Pierre Lecomte du Noüy suggests. But—his ultimate purpose? I do not think anyone knows more about that than I know, and I know nothing about it.

Your greatness is here and now. Your happiness is here and now. Here are some of the factors which create peace of mind. They are involved in creating money-wealth as well; but let us set that aside for the time being. Here are some peace-of-mind factors; read them carefully; note that you have met them in this book, in one form or another, and note that you have heard about them from other sources as well.

You must come to realize you have a conscience which will guide you, and stay on good terms with your conscience so it will guide you well.

You must take possession of your own mind, do your own thinking, live your own life.

You must keep yourself so busy living your own life that you will not be tempted to interfere in the lives of others.

You must learn to free your life of unnecessary encumbrances, both material and mental.

You must establish harmony in your own home and harmony with those among whom you work.

You must share your blessings with others, and do this wholeheartedly.

You must look at the realities of life as they are, not as you wish them to be, and properly evaluate them.

You must help others to find and develop their own powers to make themselves what they want to be.

Now, I did not invent these ways of winning peace of mind. They were known of old. They are the ways which have proved themselves right, strong and eternal. If I have made these ways more clear to you, and if I have given you practical ways in which to apply them, well and good; but the wisdom behind them is the gathered wisdom of mankind.

And so you have heard before of these peace-of-mind factors. Perhaps they were told to you as ways to help yourself get to Heaven. This belief leaves you up against a blank wall. I give them to you as representative of the tried and true methods which help you live a healthier, wealthier, better life, here, on this earth, now. Is this not sufficient?

The Creator in your life. You have seen that I do not deny the concept of a Creator as an eternal and all-pervading intelligence, or cosmic force. But the Creator with whom I made my peace many years ago does not require me to be afraid of Him; nor does He offer Himself to me merely through the intervention of any particular religion.

My Creator gave me His greatest blessing when He made me human.

He gave me the power to choose between good and bad, and made my concept as wide as all the affairs of the world and all its people. He set me at large upon the world to learn that my good deeds are rewarded in kind, and my bad deeds are just as inexorably made to draw penalties according to their nature. He gave me a mind beyond the mind of any other of His creatures, and He made me free to use my mind as only a human being can use his mind-power.

I can pray, and in constructive prayer that does not amount to begging for special favours. I can find faith which vastly enlarges my powers. Yet always I know I am the master of my fate, I am the captain of my soul, for so my Creator made me, and so I need not call upon Him constantly for guidance. Have you ever noticed that the one who does the praying very often has a large part in the answering of the prayer? I allow for the prayer that goes Beyond; but I believe that many a prayer stays within the one who prays and strengthens him in his realization of his own human abilities.

The Creator's place in your life is to help you be more triumphantly your own master. The Creator made you a creature who can think for himself, be himself, believe in what he wishes to accomplish, and mightily achieve! Do less than this and you cannot possibly fulfil yourself in all your glorious humanity.

The mind of man is filled with powers to be used, not to be neglected. These powers, these blessings, either are used—and the benefits of their use shared with others—or you incur penalties for not using them.

If you needed a house, and knew how to build a house, and had all the materials you needed for building a house, and had a lot on which to build a house, and yet neglected to build a house—then you would understand your penalty as you sat exposed in the rain and the snow.

Too many of us do not use our power to gather in the wealth and peace of mind which is available all around us. Then we are penalized by poverty, by misery, by worry and ill health— and we blame everyone but ourselves.

Anything the human mind can believe, the human mind can achieve.

Believe in poverty and you will be poor.

Believe in wealth and you will be rich.

Believe in love and you will have love.

Believe in health and you will be healthy.

You have seen what lies behind these statements. It would be well to read this book again and refresh your understanding. No book can give you all its wealth at the first reading. Make friends with this book, read it again, put it away for a while, take it out and read it once more, and you will read much between the lines—and much that applies to you.

I have shared with you what may be merely words, or great wealth and contentment—depending on how you use them. I am glad I cannot force you to use the knowledge I have given you. I am glad it is up to you to improve your own life.

I leave you now with no great ceremony.

Remember: there is no good thing in the world that is not available to you if you sufficiently desire it.

And remember: no matter what others may see of your possessions after you make a great deal of money…no matter how they may respect your offices and influence and talents no matter how much they may admire your generosity, your kindliness, your willingness to live and let live…you yourself are the only one who can hold and enjoy your greatest treasure, peace of mind.

Cherish your visions and your dreams. They are the children of your soul, the blueprints of your ultimate achievements.

POINTS TO REMEMBER

1. Fear has no place in a well-lived life.
2. Peace of mind, the greatest of the riches and how to find it.
3. Find the power to turn what the human mind believes into what the human mind achieves.

2

THE BEGINNING OF ALL RICHES

The largest audience ever assembled in the history of mankind sat breathlessly awaiting the message of a mysterious man who was about to reveal to the world the secret of his riches.
In that audience were men who had tried and failed so often that they had all but lost hope!

And there were young men and young women—mere boys and girls— who were filled with hope and courage and eagerness to learn the way to riches.

There were doctors, lawyers, dentists, engineers and school teachers, waiting to hear what the speaker might have to say which would put them on the road to riches.

Clergymen of every religion on earth were there, with the hope that they might gather from the message of the speaker some inspirational ideas they could pass on to the members of their congregations.

Newspaper reporters were more numerous than bees; a great battery of cameras trained upon the speaker's platform, and the newsreel men were present with their moving picture cameras and sound equipment.

There were taxicab drivers, mechanics, bricklayers, merchants, barbers and newsboys, representing every trade and every calling on earth, and many of them had come from distant places.

Slowly the curtain began to rise, the Chairman walking to the speaker's dais raised his hand for silence! The noise died down and a silent hush spread over the great audience.

The introduction of the speaker was brief. The Chairman simply said, 'Ladies and Gentlemen, I have the honour to introduce to you the richest man in all the world. He has come to tell you about the MASTER-KEY TO RICHES.'

The speaker walked briskly to the speaker's dais.

He was dressed in a long black robe and wore a mask over his eyes.

His hair was of a greyish tint, and he appeared to be about sixty years of age.

He stood silently for a few moments, while the cameras flashed. Then, speaking slowly, in a voice soft and pleasing, like music, he began his message,

'You have come here to seek the MASTER-KEY TO RICHES!

'You have come because of that human urge for the better things in life, which is the common desire of all people.

'You desire economic security which money alone can provide.

'Some of you desire an outlet for your talents in order that you may have the joy of creating your own riches.

'Some of you are seeking the easy way to riches, with the hope that you will find it without giving anything in return; that too is a common desire. But it is a desire I shall hope to modify for your benefit, as from experience I have learned that there is no such thing as something for nothing.'

'There is but one sure way to riches, and that may be attained only by those who have the MASTER-KEY TO RICHES!

'This MASTER-KEY is an ingenious device with which those who possess it may unlock the door to the solution of all of their problems. Its powers of magic transcend those of the famous Aladdin's Lamp.

'It opens the door to sound health.

'It opens the door to love and romance.

'It opens the door to friendship, by revealing the traits of personality and character which make enduring friends.

'It reveals the method by which every adversity, every failure, every disappointment, every mistaken error of judgment and every past defeat may be transmuted into riches of a priceless value.

'It kindles anew the dead hopes of all who possess it, and it reveals the formula by which one may "tune in" and draw upon the great reservoir of Infinite Intelligence, through that state of mind known as Faith.

'It lifts humble men to positions of power, fame and fortune.

'It turns back the hands of the clock of Time and renews the spirit of youth for those who have grown old too soon.

'It provides the method by which one may take full and complete possession of one's own mind, thus giving one unchallengeable control over the emotions of the heart and the power of thinking.

'It bridges the deficiencies of those who have inadequate education through formal schooling, and puts them substantially on the same plane of opportunity that is enjoyed by those who have a better education.

'And lastly, it opens the doors, one by one, to the Twelve Great Riches of Life, which I shall presently describe for you in detail.

'Listen carefully to what I have to say, for I shall not pass this way again. Listen not only with open ears, but with open minds and eager hearts, remembering that no man may hear that for which he has not the preparation for hearing.

'The preparation consists of many things, among them sincerity of purpose, humility of heart, a full recognition of the truth that no man knows everything; that the combined knowledge of mankind has not been enough to save men from cutting one another to pieces through warfare, nor to restrain them from cheating and stealing the fruits of labour from their fellowmen.

'I shall speak to you of facts and describe to you many principles of which many of you may never have heard, for they are known only to those who have prepared themselves to accept the MASTER-KEY—a small but ever-increasing number of people who have attained the Degree of Fellowship.

'The Fellowship is made up of men and women from many walks of life, of all nationalities and creeds. Its purpose is to reveal to mankind the benefits which are available through the spirit of the Brotherhood of man.

'The Fellowship was born of the necessity of rehabilitating a war-worn world into which civilization was brought to the very brink of destruction through World War II. The Fellowship is non-sectarian and non-commercial.

'Its members work individually. It has no authorized leaders, but everyone who qualifies for the Degree of Fellowship becomes a leader unto himself.

'The only condition that is required for membership is that all who qualify for the degree shall share with others the benefits they receive through the MASTER-KEY TO RICHES—as many others as they may find who are willing to prepare themselves to receive the benefits.

'The Fellowship prepares men and women to relate themselves to one another as brothers and sisters.

'It recognizes the great abundance of material riches available for mankind and provides a rational plan by which every person may share in these riches in proportion to his talents, as they are expressed through useful service.

'It frowns upon the idea of too much for the few and too little for the many, but it also discourages all who endeavour to get something for nothing. And it discourages the accumulation of riches by individuals whose greed inspires them to seek more than they can use for their own economic security and to provide opportunities through which others may attain such security.

'The Fellowship has a stupendous task ahead of it.

'Civilization must live and go forward, not backward, for that is the plan of the Creator of all things.

'Men must learn to live together as brothers, so that they may walk arm in arm, do the world's work and reap their just reward without poverty, without hardship, without fear or trembling.

'The members of the Fellowship have learned to do this without suffering the loss of any of the joys of living or sacrificing any of their rights as individuals. Nay, they have discovered that the Fellowship way is the only path to enduring happiness.

'I have come to tell you about the Fellowship and to place in your hands the MASTER-KEY to all riches.

'My identity will not be revealed, for it would be of no benefit to you. If you wish to speak of me you may call me the "Rich Man from Happy Valley."'

THE DUAL SELF

'Before I describe the Twelve Great Riches let me reveal to you some of the riches you already possess; riches of which most of you may not be conscious.

'First, I would have you recognize that each of you is a plural personality, although you may regard yourself as a single personality. You and every other person consist of at least two distinct personalities, and many of you possess more.

'There is that self which you recognize when you look into a mirror. That is your physical self. But it is only the house in which your other selves live. In that house there are two individuals at least who are eternally in conflict with each other.

'One is a negative sort of person who thinks and moves and lives in an atmosphere of fear and doubt and poverty and ill health. This self expects failure, and seldom is disappointed. It thinks of the circumstances of life which you do not want but which you seem forced to accept—poverty, greed, superstition, fear, doubt, worry and physical sickness.

'And one is your "other self", a positive sort of person who thinks in terms of opulence, sound health, love and friendship, personal achievement, creative vision, service to others and who guides you unerringly to the attainment of all of these blessings. It is this self which alone is capable of recognizing and appropriating the Twelve Great Riches. It is the only self which is capable of receiving the Master-Key to Riches.

'These are not imaginary personalities of which I speak. They are real, for they have been revealed through scientific investigation of irreproachable authenticity.

'Then you have many other priceless assets of which you may not be aware; hidden riches you have neither recognized nor used. Among these is a modern radio broadcasting and receiving station so powerful that it may pick up and send out the vibrations of thought from or to any part of the world, including the potential capacity to reach out into the cosmos and tune in with the power of Infinite Intelligence.

'Your radio station operates automatically and continuously, when you are asleep just as when you are awake.

'And it is under the control at all times of one or the other of your two major personalities, the negative personality or the positive personality. When your negative personality is in control, your radio station picks up only the negative thought vibrations which are being sent out by hundreds of millions of other negative personalities throughout the world. These are accepted, acted upon and translated into their physical equivalent in terms of the circumstances of life which you do not wish.

'When your positive personality is in control it picks up only the positive thought vibrations being released by millions of other positive personalities throughout the world, and translates them into their physical equivalent in terms of prosperity, sound health, love, hope, faith, peace of mind and happiness; the values of life for which you and every other normal person are searching.

'I have come to reveal to you the Master-Key by which you may attain these and many other riches. That mysterious key which unlocks the doors to the solution of all human problems, acquires all riches, and places every individual radio station under the control of one's "other self."

'I am known as the Rich Man from Happy Valley because I have come into possession of the Master-Key to Riches. The nature of my riches I shall presently reveal to you. But first let me tell you that I was not born to riches.

'I was born in poverty and illiteracy.

'My formal education has been limited to the knowledge available through a country grade school.

'And the entire universe, as far as I was concerned, extended no further than the boundary lines of the backwoods county into which I was born.

'Then came a great awakening. Love came into my heart, and with it the influence of the greatest person I shall ever hope to know. She became my wife and guide, for she came from the outer world—that world I had not suspected to exist. She was a woman of culture and education. From her I learned some of the secrets of biology, and chemistry, and astronomy, and physics. She reached deeply into my soul and uncovered that "other self" of which I had no knowledge.

'Step by step, patiently and with love, she lifted me into a higher and yet higher plane of understanding, until at long last I was prepared to receive the great Master-Key to Riches—the gift which I shall share with you in the hope that you may become as rich as I.

With that blessing came also a responsibility consisting of an obligation to reveal the secrets of the great Master-Key to as many of you as may prepare yourselves to receive it. But let me here warn you that the Master-Key may be retained only by those who accept the obligation to share it with others. No man may use it selfishly, for his personal aggrandizement alone.

'I shall reveal to you the means by which you may share the blessings of the Master-Key, but the responsibility of sharing must become your own.

'The founders of the Rotary Club movement must have recognized the benefits of sharing, for they adopted as their motto, "*He profits most who serves best.*"

'And every close observer must have recognized that all individual successes which endure *have had their beginning through the beneficent influence of some other individual*, through some form of sharing.

'My great opportunity consisted in the willingness of my wife to share with me the knowledge which she had acquired, plus the knowledge I gained from the principles which placed the Master-Key within my reach.

'Your opportunity may well consist in my willingness to share this knowledge with you. But I have not come to give you material riches alone. I have come to share with you the knowledge by which you may acquire riches—*all riches*—through the expression of *your own personal initiative!*

'That is the greatest of all gifts!

'And it is the only kind of gift that anyone who is blessed with the advantages of a great nation like ours should expect. For here we have every potential form of riches available to mankind. We have them in great abundance.

'So I assume that you too wish to become rich.

'Let us become partners in the attainment of your desire, for I have found the way to all riches. Therefore I am prepared to serve as your guide.

'I sought the path to riches the hard way before I learned that there is a short and dependable path I could have followed had I been guided as I hope to guide you.

'Before we begin our journey to the land of riches let us take inventory so that we may know the true nature of riches. Yes, let us be prepared to recognize riches when we come within their reach.

'Some believe that riches consist in money alone!

'But enduring riches, in the broader sense, consist in many other values than those of material things, and may I add that without these other intangible values the possession of money will not bring the happiness which some believe it will provide.

'When I speak of "riches" I have in mind the greater riches whose possessors have made life pay off on their own terms—the terms of full and complete happiness. I call these the "*Twelve Riches of Life*". And I sincerely wish to share them with all of you who are prepared to receive them, in whole or in part.

'You may wonder about my willingness to share, so I shall tell you that the MASTER-KEY TO RICHES enables its possessors to add to their own store of riches everything of value which they share with others.

'This is one of the strangest facts of life, but it is a fact which each of you must recognize and respect if you hope to become as rich as I.'

POINTS TO REMEMBER

1. How to take full and complete possession of one's own mind.
2. The twelve great riches of life.
3. The fellowship way is the only path to enduring happiness.

3

THE ATTITUDE THAT BRINGS WEALTH AND PEACE OF MIND

A life of wealth enjoyed by a mind at peace comes most often to men who maintain a positive mental attitude. With definiteness of purpose you add great positive power to your own mental attitude, and you can use definite motives to sustain the actions which propel you toward your goal. At the same time you can set up spiritual guardians to keep your attitudes at a high 'Yes' level, avoid conflicts of motive, tune-in on other positive minds.

The computers which are beginning to manage our world are complicated devices. Most of them, however, have a very simple basic principle: they say Yes or No. They either open a kind of electrical gate or they keep it closed, and by multiplying this process they can assimilate and select all kinds of information.

The mind of man is far more wonderful than any machine. Within it, however, there seems to be a kind of Yes-No valve at the focal point of thinking. It is as though your awareness of a circumstance of life—sent to your brain by your sight, hearing and other senses—presents itself at the Yes-No point to be processed. A person who maintains a positive attitude will find every possible Yes in that circumstance and make it part of his life. A person who maintains a negative mental attitude will lean toward the No side, miss much that is good, live with much that is painful and damaging.

Nothing but a mental attitude? Nothing but a mental attitude, but it is right there that your success or your failure, your peace of mind or your nervous tension, your tendency toward good health or your tendency toward illness begins.

Fortunately it is possible for anyone to make the change from negativism to positivism, and thus basically condition his brain to bring all that is good in life. Moreover, there are certain 'control levers' which the Creator makes available to us, and it is easy to see how successful people use these levers, once you know what they are.

I shall give you some here and some in other chapters so as to reinforce your memory. Now and then you will find repetition of names, facts and methods in this books, always with a view toward helping you remember.

Control your mental attitude with definiteness of purpose. Emerson said, 'The world makes way for a man who knows where he is going.'

Think what it means to know where you are going! Automatically you rid yourself of all kinds of fears and doubts which may have crept into the making-up-your-mind process. Your purpose is definite and—presto!—all the limitless forces of your mind focus upon that purpose and no other. Knowing your purpose, you cannot be led astray by circumstances or words which have nothing to do with your purpose. Where, before, a day's work may have contained a good deal of wasted motion, now your efforts are lined up so that each mental or physical motion helps every other motion.

You can see the connection with building wealth, for work

done well is a basic wealth-builder. Now see the connection with peace of mind. A man who works wholeheartedly at his job is not concerned with such matters as finding fault with others, disturbing his conscience by cutting corners in his work, watching the clock and so forth. Nor will he be discouraged by any obstacles which may crop up; his positive and focused mental attitude keeps him in a prime position to handle problems and overcome them.

EFFICIENCY AND POSITIVITY

Is this a secret of 'genius'? I have mentioned that many eminently successful men do not possess any greater intelligence than most other men possess. Yet their achievements are such that we may say that these men have 'genius'. Surely it is the positive mental attitude of these men which makes their brain-power, not greater, but more efficient and more available than most others'. When I spoke to such men as Henry Ford, Andrew Carnegie and Thomas A. Edison, I spoke with minds free of any fear or doubt that they could do anything they wished to do.

I know that Andrew Carnegie was well aware of the need for a positive mental attitude. Before he undertook to back me in my success, he really put me 'on the spot' as to my mental attitude.

Looking at me shrewdly across his desk, that canny Scot said, 'We've talked a long time and I have shown you the greatest opportunity a young man ever had to become famous, rich and useful. Now—if I choose you out of the two hundred and forty other applicants for this job—if I introduce you to the outstandingly successful men in America—if I help you get their collaboration in finding out the true philosophy of success—will you devote twenty years to the job, earning your own living as you go along? We have had sufficient discussion. I want your answer—yes or no.'

I began to think of all the obstacles that would stand in my way. I began to think of all the hurdles I would have to jump. I began to think of all the time I would have to spend, and the big job of writing, and the problem of earning my living all that while—and so forth.

I spent twenty-nine seconds struggling with a negative mental attitude which, had it overcome me, would have affected me negatively ever after.

How do I know I took just twenty-nine seconds? Because, when I found the positive mental attitude which I had lost temporarily, and said 'Yes!'—Mr Carnegie showed me the stopwatch he had been holding beneath his desk. He had given me just one minute in which to show my positive state of mind otherwise, he felt, he would not have been able to depend on it. I had beaten the deadline by just thirty-one seconds, and thereby embraced an opportunity that was destined to change and improve the lives of millions of people, including my own.

A positive mind tunes in on other positive minds. Once I had accepted that great task and had set my mind confidently toward it, I found that my imagined obstacles simply melted away. Of course my positive mental attitude helped me not only in finding out the success secrets of some five hundred of America's wealthiest men, but also in making considerably more than a mere living. Am I a genius? I must say I have positive evidence I am not!

In meeting many men I discovered a very valuable fact: a positive mind automatically obtains benefit from other positive minds.

Are you aware of the general principle of radio broadcasting?

It is this: when electrical vibrations of rapid frequency are impressed upon a wire, those vibrations leap into space. Another wire far away—the receiving antenna—can pick them up, and thus a message or a picture is transmitted over thousands of miles, or millions of miles in space-age communication.

There are electrical currents in the brain. They give you a private broadcasting station through which you may send out any kind of thought vibrations you desire. Keep that station busy sending out thoughts of a positive nature, thoughts which will benefit others, and you will find you can receive kindred thought vibrations from other minds whose attitude is tuned to yours.

When I visited such successful men as those I have mentioned, and many others such as John Wanamaker, Frank A. Vanderlip, Edward Bok and Woodrow Wilson, both they and I felt the attunement of mind to mind. Otherwise I surely would have met with opposition when I asked those top-ranking men to give me of their time and experience. Not only did such men spend hours talking to me, but also they served as my teachers and guides for year after year, and charged me nothing.

Believe in what you are doing, and you too will see the great effect of your belief upon those whom you may request to help you. Doubt yourself and the No part of your mind takes over and draws defeat instead of victory.

This barely sketches in the all-pervasive power of a positive mental attitude. Let us look at some of the other 'control levers' which combine with a positive mental attitude to give you wealth and peace of mind for an entire, victorious lifetime.

The nine major motives. It is not for nothing that court trials often concern themselves with questions of motive. Everything you do is the result of one or more motives. In various combinations we use nine basic motives. The seven positive motives are:

1. The emotion of LOVE
2. The emotion of SEX
3. The desire for MATERIAL GAIN
4. The desire for SELF-PRESERVATION
5. The desire for FREEDOM OF BODY AND MIND
6. The desire for SELF-EXPRESSION
7. The desire for PERPETUATION OF LIFE AFTER DEATH

The two negative emotions are:

1. The emotion of ANGER AND REVENGE
2. The emotion of FEAR

In those nine motives you can find the roots of everything you do or refrain from doing. Peace of mind is attained only by the exercise of the seven positive motives as a general pattern of life. Rarely if ever does a person who has peace of mind exercise the two negative motives or emotions. You cannot have peace of mind while you fear anything or anyone. You cannot have peace of mind while you entertain the kind of anger which brings you to a desire for revenge or a desire to injure another, no matter what the justification may seem to be.

THE PRICE OF PEACE OF MIND

Great men have no time to waste with a desire to injure others. If they did, they would not be great men. Great men are not immune to fear, but theirs is not the kind of fear that hangs on constantly and takes over all of life. Look to small, mean men to see lifelong patterns of fear and anger. Their minds are so filled with these negative influences that they cannot find the power to shape the circumstances they desire.

Recently I heard about a man, now seventy, who fifteen years ago lost all his money in a real estate venture. Taking the advice of a friend, he had borrowed heavily in order to invest in vacant swampland on the assumption that in a couple of years the land would be in great demand for building lots. This did not transpire, the man's notes became due, and he had to see his retail shoe business sold out from under him.

The friend who had badly advised him also had lost money. Nevertheless this man became filled with hatred toward his friend and said he would get even 'if it's the last thing I do'. It nearly was. Five years of hatred left him incapable even of doing business. Meanwhile the friend prospered and seemed far out of reach of any puny revenge. The man who had lost his money at length lost the balance wheel of his mind and had to spend six months in a quiet place in the country surrounded by a high wall.

In his last month of confinement, however, he was sufficiently recovered to listen to an adviser who pointed out to him that hatred and the desire for revenge had done him far more harm than had been done by his losing his money. He was persuaded to forgive the friend who had led him into the real estate deal. He even wrote to this man, telling of his change of heart.

When he went back into business it was with love of his fellow men and the determination to keep his mind filled with positive, constructive motives. Beginning at the age of sixty, he built a new career. Now, at seventy, he is fairly well off, and most of all he has peace of mind, the one form of wealth which is indispensable.

I myself have suffered from the effects of negative motives from time to time. When I went into hiding, as discussed in the last chapter, I acted at first upon a very wise motive of self-preservation. Soon, however, this turned into fear and with the fear came misery. Fortunately I saw in time what was happening to me. It cannot happen again.

You can make yourself aware of certain principles of personal guidance and guardianship; and to make these principles real and memorable, you can personalize them—see them as so many Princes in armour who stand at the doors of your mind. These Princes challenge every thought-vibration which seeks to enter. They keep your mind positive, effective and free of discord. I shall name my own Princes, a list which you may wish to modify to suit your own life-requirements.

The Prince of Peace of Mind. He stands at the very outer door and asks all callers if they come in peace to share my peace. If not, they are turned away.

The Prince of Hope and Faith. He admits only those influences which keep my mind alerted with belief in my mission in life.

The Prince of Love and Romance. He brings into my mind only those influences which keep love eternally fresh in my heart.

The Prince of Sound Physical Health. He knows the kind of mental influences which can destroy health, and admits only those states of mind which help the body maintain its vigour.

The Prince of Financial Security. When I desire him to stand on guard, he admits no thoughts save those which bring me worthy financial benefit.

The Prince of Overall Wisdom. He is charged with passing certain thoughts into my store of knowledge when he sees they will benefit me or help me benefit others.

The Prince of Patience. He keeps away all impulses to rush, to tackle jobs half-prepared, to be in any way impatient with the power of time.

The Prince of Normhill. 'Normhill' is a very personal word I have created for my own use. Combining certain names, it means to me what it cannot mean to any other. Just so, create your own name for your own very personal Prince. This Prince stands guard along with all the others. The others from time to time may be relieved of duty; for instance, one hardly may wish continually to keep out all thoughts except those which have to do with financial security. Your special personal Prince is always there, representing all the special personal influences in your life. Normhill is my ambassador-at-large who performs services not assigned to the other members of my invisible family of guides.

When you have made yourself well aware of your corps of spiritual Princes, they serve to rally all your forces to solve any problem or to set up special lines of defence.

Sometimes I find myself talking to someone whose antagonistic attitude begins to invade my peace of mind. Very well—I send a special alert to the Prince of Peace of Mind. Immediately he takes charge of the ramparts with doubled strength, and I am calm and in control of my own mind once more.

Or, let us say, I feel some physical ache or pain. I call upon the Prince of Sound Physical Health to look into the cause, and I get good results. I believe I have received benefits of healing which are beyond the power of ordinary medical science to explain.

My Princes of Guidance receive a certain compensation for their services. Their 'pay' is my eternal gratitude. Daily I express this gratitude, first to each of the Princes individually, then to all of them in their mighty group. You will find this expression of gratitude of great help in keeping your mind alerted to its own powers. I know that if I ever neglect it, I feel a neglect on the part of my Princes. When, once again, I make myself aware every day that I have great spiritual forces at my command—there they are once more, as strong as ever.

Don't let the motive of material gain conflict with the motive of freedom. Freedom of body is easy to see and understand; but freedom of mind is a subtle matter. Fear and anger put the mind behind bars. Guilt wraps the mind in chains. To add a bit of levity to a serious matter: once there was a man who was encouraged to know himself. Immediately he handcuffed himself to his bed, so he would not get up and rifle his own pockets during the night.

All too often the motive of material gain—excellent in itself—conflicts with the excellent motive of freedom of body and mind because in gaining what is material we give up freedom of mind; we load the mind with guilt and fear because we do not act honestly.

In addition, one who makes his money through taking dishonest advantage of his fellow men has cheated himself of the genuine joy which comes with honest success. When you obey the rules of a game, and win, you have done something for your soul. When you cheat and win, you only call it winning, but you have really lost instead.

I believe I was fortunate in starting my career very early in life, so that I learned life's lessons quite early. Let me tell you of an experience I had while I was holding my first job. I was just out of business college and I was inexperienced in the ways of life and the character of men.

My employer owned a number of banks. He had placed his son as a cashier of one of his banks, in a distant town. One night a hotel manager in that town telephoned me, saying my employer's son was in serious difficulty. He had not been able to reach my employer. Immediately, I boarded the train and arrived in the town early the next morning.

When I went to the bank I found the door closed but unlocked. Inside, I discovered that the vault had been left open and beautiful green currency was scattered all over the teller's counter.

I closed the door and picked up the telephone. I managed to get my employer on the phone and told him why I had gone to that town and what I had found on my arrival. In great distress, he said, 'Go ahead and count the money. Balance the books. Draw a draft on me for whatever shortage there may be.'

I settled down to counting the money. To my great surprise, not a cent was missing.

I sat there looking at those piles of greenbacks. My youth had been tragic, turbulent and poor. My present state was one of bare solvency. I sat there looking at nearly $50,000 in cash, knowing that I could put at least half of it into my pocket and nobody would be the wiser. My employer's son showed obvious signs of mental instability. Everyone would assume he had taken the money. He even had acted as though he had filled his own pockets—and I was the only one who knew he had not.

The motive of material gain nudged heavily at me. But the motive of freedom said: don 't do it. Or rather, it was 'something' that kept me honest, for at that time I could not have named the major motives. Perhaps that 'something' was the result of certain sessions I had had with my stepmother before I had left home, in which she had instilled into me the fact that I was in control of my own mind and that always I must live with myself.

I locked the money into the vault forthwith, then phoned my employer and told him there was no deficiency to make up; not a cent had been stolen. I walked out of that bank with a mind at peace, a mind that was free and joyously positive.

Forever after I have placed the motive of freedom ahead

of the motive of material gain. I have succeeded in having all the money I need without ever hampering either my inward or outward freedom.

LIFE IS A MIRROR

This episode was one of several which led me straight to Andrew Carnegie and my realization of my goal in life. My employer was grateful for the way in which I had protected his son's reputation as best I could. He was responsible later for my entering Georgetown University Law School. This led through a chain of circumstances to my assignment to interview Mr Carnegie. If I had yielded to the material gain motive that day in the bank, the Science of Personal Achievement might never have come into being.

Yes, as Emerson suggested, there is a silent partner in all our transactions, and woe is the lot of the man who tries to drive a sharp bargain with Life.

Life reflects your own thoughts back to you. Thoughts are things, a poet said, and truly they have an existence of their own, so that a curse comes back to curse you and a blessing comes back to bless you, reflected by the mighty mirror of life. Another poet said, 'I am the master of my fate, I am the captain of my soul.' This too is true, and the two truths harmonize. Send out positive thoughts from a positively oriented soul and the world will reflect back greater and greater positive influences to help you.

Turn back and read the list of nine basic motives. Concentrate on the seven positive motives. Remember it is possible for these motives to come into conflict, as we have seen; but by and large they drive one way, and with a positive mental attitude they take you the way you want to go. We shall not say farewell to the motives till we are finished with this book; but let us now pay our respects briefly.

Love has limitless scope. Handle it in a spirit of reverence, for it is tuned to the Eternal. Give freely of it and you will attract as much as or more than you give; stop giving love and you stop receiving. With no other emotion or motive or desire is the mirror of life so very evident.

Sex is the great creative force of the universe. On its highest plane it merges with love; but love can exist without being sexual. The mighty power of sex can be transmuted into action for the achievement of profound purpose, and so important is the this matter that later on we shall devote an entire chapter to it. On the other hand, sex may be debauched and misused, and it is in this guise that it brings grief and trouble to mankind and gives itself an underserved bad reputation.

Self-preservation can become a negative force when one seeks it without regard to the rights of other people. It is instilled by Nature to help us stay alive. Even so, the human being assumes the prerogative of rising above it. When a ship is sinking it is women and children first, and there are many parallel instances which call forth a nobility in human nature.

Self-expression is part of finding one's self. It is part of one's freedom to be one's self. Thus it is positive, constructive and infinitely valuable. Only make sure that your own means of self-expression do not demean or damage others.

Perpetuation of life after death belongs among the earliest beliefs and motives of mankind. It should be bounded by common sense and a true understanding of one's relationship to that change known as death. When wrapped in superstition and fear, this motive leads only to wretchedness. It can turn life into a preparation for death and hamper an entire civilization.

The surest way of finding peace of mind. The surest way of

finding peace of mind is that which helps the greatest number of others to find it.

Let this be your guide to your use of the great motivating forces; then you will know you are using them correctly, not corrupting them.

Is there peace of mind in prayer? There can be. There should be. But note how many people go to prayer only in the hour of a misfortune, when the motive of fear dominates their minds. The approach must be negative in that case, and so, in terms of peace of mind, the results must be negative as well.

Prayers which bring peace of mind proceed from a mind which gives forth a confident message even though that mind may be afflicted with problems and sorrow. Prayers which free great forces to solve problems are born in minds which know that the problems can be solved once the forces are found—and have perfect confidence in the existence of those forces.

Along with many others I see evidence of an Intelligence beyond man's. I believe that the positively conditioned mind may at times tune in on that Intelligence. Yet mind-conditioning through prayer or resolution is something an individual must accomplish for himself. When the Creator made man free to seek his own destiny, and choose between good and evil, he gave man this prerogative as well. Every great accomplishment of any man at any time first had to exist as a thought before it could exist as reality.

Have you recognized the Supreme Secret?

POINTS TO REMEMBER

1. A life of wealth is only enjoyed by someone who possess a positive mental attitude.
2. Control your mental attitude with definiteness of purpose.
3. The nine basic motives for any human endeavour.

4

SPECIALIZED KNOWLEDGE

There are two kinds of knowledge. One is general; the other, specialized. General knowledge, no matter how great in quantity or varietyit may be, is of but little use in the accumulation of money. The faculties of the great universities possess, in the aggregate, practically every form of general knowledge known to civilization. *Most of the professors have not amassed great wealth!* They specialize in *teaching* knowledge, but they do not specialize in the organization or the *use* of knowledge for the accumulation of money.

KNOWLEDGE will not attract money (or any other kind of success) unless it is organized and intelligently directed, through practical PLANS OF ACTION, to the DEFINITE END of accumulating money. Lack of understanding of this fact has been the source of confusion to millions of people who falsely believe that 'knowledge is power'. It is nothing of the sort! Knowledge is only *potential* power. It becomes power only when, and if, it is organized into definite plans of action and directed to a definite end.

This 'missing link; in all systems of education known to civilization today may be found in the failure of educational institutions to teach their students HOW TO ORGANIZE AND USE KNOWLEDGE AFTER THEYACQUIRE IT.

Many people make the mistake of assuming that because Henry Ford had but little schooling, he was not educated. Those who make this mistake did not know Henry Ford, nor do they understand the real meaning of the word 'educate'. The word is derived from the Latin word *educo*, meaning to *educe*, to draw out, to DEVELOP FROM WITHIN.

An educated person is not necessarily one who has an abundance of general or specialized knowledge. To be truly educated is to have so developed the faculties of mind that one may acquire anything one wishes, or its equivalent, without violating the rights of others. Henry Ford comes well within the meaning of this definition.

During World War I, a Chicago newspaper published certain editorials in which, among other statements, Henry Ford was called 'an ignorant pacifist'. Mr Ford objected to the statements and brought suit against the paper for libeling him. When the suit was tried in the courts, the attorneys for the paper pleaded justification and placed Mr Ford himself on the witness stand for the purpose of proving to the jury that he was ignorant. The attorneys asked Mr Ford a great variety of questions, all of them intended to prove by his own evidence that, while he might possess considerable specialized knowledge pertaining to the manufacture of automobiles, he was, in the main, ignorant.

Mr Ford was plied with such questions as the following, 'Who was Benedict Arnold?' and 'How many soldiers did the British send over to America to put down the Rebellion of 1776?' In answer to the last question, Mr Ford replied, 'I do not know the exact number of soldiers the British sent over, but I have heard that it was a considerably larger number than ever went back.'

Finally, Mr Ford became tired of this line of questioning,

and in reply to a particularly offensive question, he leaned over, pointed his finger at the lawyer who had asked the question, and said, 'If I should really WANT to answer the foolish question you have just asked or any of the other questions you have been asking me, let me remind you that I have a row of electric push-buttons on my desk, and by pushing the right button, I can summon to my aid men who can answer ANY question I desire to ask concerning the business to which I am devoting most of my efforts. Now, will you kindly tell me WHY I should clutter up my mind with general knowledge for the purpose of being able to answer questions when I have men around me who can supply any knowledge I require?'

There certainly was good logic to that reply. The answer floored the lawyer. Every person in the courtroom realized it was the answer not of an ignorant man, but of a man of EDUCATION. Any person is educated who knows where to get knowledge when it is needed and how to organize that knowledge into definite plans of action. Through the assistance of his Master Mind Group, Henry Ford had at his command all the specialized knowledge he needed to enable him to become one of the wealthiest individuals in America. *It was not essential that he have this knowledge in his own mind.* Surely no person who has sufficient inclination and intelligence to read a book of this nature can possibly miss the significance of this illustration.

SPECIALIZED KNOWLEDGE

Before you can be sure of your ability to transmute DESIRE into its monetary equivalent, you will require SPECIALIZED KNOWLEDGE of the service, merchandise or profession which you intend to offer in return for fortune. Perhaps you may need much more specialized knowledge than you have the ability or the inclination to acquire, and if this should be true, you may bridge your weakness through the aid of your Master Mind Group. Andrew Carnegie stated that he personally knew nothing about the technical end of the steel business. Moreover, he did not particularly care to know anything about it. The specialized knowledge which he required for the manufacture and marketing of steel he found available through the individual units of his MASTER MIND GROUP.

The accumulation of great fortunes calls for POWER, and power is acquired through highly organized and intelligently directed specialized knowledge, but that knowledge does not necessarily have to be in the possession of the person who accumulates the fortune.

The preceding paragraph should give hope and encouragement to the person who has ambition to accumulate a fortune, but who does not have the necessary education to supply such specialized knowledge as may be required. People sometimes go through life suffering from inferiority complexes because they are not 'well educated'. Yet, the individual who can organize and direct a Master Mind Group of people who possess knowledge useful in the accumulation of money is just as educated as anyone in the group. REMEMBER THAT if you suffer from a feeling of inferiority because your schooling has been limited.

Thomas A. Edison had only three months of formal education during his entire life. Yet he did not lack education, nor did he die poor.

Henry Ford had less than a sixth grade schooling, but he managed to do pretty well by himself financially.

SPECIALIZED KNOWLEDGE is among the most

plentiful and the cheapest forms of service which may be had! If you doubt this, consult the payroll of any college or university.

IT PAYS TO KNOW HOW TO PURCHASE KNOWLEDGE

First of all, decide the sort of specialized knowledge you require and the purpose for which it is needed. To a large extent, your major purpose in life, the goal toward which you are working, will help determine what knowledge you need. With this question settled, your next move requires that you have accurate information concerning dependable sources of knowledge. The more important of these are:

- (a) your own experience and education
- (b) experience and education available through cooperation ofothers (Master Mind Alliance)
- (c) colleges and universities
- (d) public libraries (through books and periodicals in which maybe found all the knowledge organized by civilization)
- (e) special training courses (through night schools and homestudy materials in particular)

As knowledge is acquired, it must be organized and put into use, for a definite purpose, through practical plans. Knowledge has no value except that which can be gained from its application toward some worthy end. Thisis one reason why a college degree in itself is not valued more highly. It often represents nothing but miscellaneous knowledge.

If you contemplate pursuing additional formal education, first determine the purpose for which you want the knowledge you are seeking, then learn where this particular sort of knowledge can be obtained from reliable sources.

Successful people, in all callings, never stop acquiring specialized knowledge related to their major purpose, business or profession. Those who are not successful usually make the mistake of believing that the 'knowledge-acquiring' period ends when one finishes school. The truth is that formal education does but little more than to put one in the way of learning how to acquire practical knowledge.

We find ourselves in a Changed World today, and we have also seen some astounding changes in educational requirements. The order of the day is SPECIALIZATION. This truth was emphasized by Robert P. Moore, quoted in a piece written when he was an administrator at Columbia University:

Specialists Most Sought
Particularly sought after by employing companies are candidates who have specialized in some field—business school graduates with training in accounting and statistics, engineers of all varieties, journalists, architects, chemists and also outstanding leaders…of the senior class.

The [graduate] who has been active on the campus, whose personality is such that he or she gets along with all kinds of people and who has done an adequate job with studies has a most decided edge over the strictly academic student. Some of these, because of their all-around qualifications, have received several offers of positions, a few of them as many as six.

In departing from the conception that the 'straight A' student was invariably the one to get the choice of the better jobs, Mr Moore said that most companies look not only to academic records but to activity records and personalities of the students.

One of the largest industrial companies, the leader in itsfield, in writing to Mr Moore concerning prospective seniors at the college, said, 'We are interested primarily in finding people who can makeexceptional progress in management work. For this reason we emphasize qualities of character, intelligence and personality far more than specific educational background.'

APPRENTICESHIP PROPOSED

Proposing a system of 'apprenticing' students in offices, stores and industrial occupations during the summer vacation, Mr Moore asserts that after the first two or three years of college, every student should be asked 'to choose a definite future course and to call a halt if the student has been merely pleasantly drifting without purpose through an unspecialized academic curriculum. Colleges and universities must face the practical consideration that all professions and occupations now demand specialists,' he said, urging that educational institutions accept more direct responsibility for vocational guidance.

One of the most reliable and practical sources of knowledge available to those who need specialized training is the night schools operated in most large cities. And correspondence schools give specialized training anywherethe U.S. mails go, on all subjects that can be taught by the extension method. America is also blessed with an abundance of self-study books, courses and other materials which one may use to acquire specialized training and knowledge. One advantage, in particular, of self-study training is the flexibility of the study program which permits one to study during spare time, during work breaks, or during travel.

Anything acquired without effort and without cost is generally unappreciated, often discredited. Perhaps this is why we get so little from our marvelous opportunity in public schools. The SELF-DISCIPLINE one receives from a definite program of specialized study makes up, to some extent, for the wasted opportunity when knowledge was available without cost.

I learned this from experience early in my career. I enrolled for a home study course in advertising. After completing eight or ten lessons I stopped studying, but the school did not stop sending me bills. Moreover, it insisted upon payment whether I kept up my studies or not. I decided that if I had to pay for the course (which I had legally obligated myself to do), I should complete the lessons and get my money's worth. I felt at the time that the collection system of the school was somewhat too well organized, but I learned later in life that it was a valuable part of my training for which no charge had been made. Being forced to pay, I went ahead and completed the course. Later in life I discovered that the efficient collection system of that school had been worth much to me in the form of money I would later earn because of the training in advertising I had so reluctantly taken.

We have in this country the greatest public school system in the world. We have invested fabulous sums for fine buildings. We have provided convenient transportation for children living in rural and other areas. But there is one astounding weakness to this marvelous system—IT IS FREE! One of the strange things about human beings is that they value only that which has a price. The free schools of America and the free public libraries do not impress people *because they are free* (or appear to be so). This is the major reason why so many people find it necessary to acquire additional training after they quit school and go to work. It is also one of the major reasons why EMPLOYERS GIVE GREATER CONSIDERATION TO EMPLOYEES WHO PARTICIPATE REGULARLY IN SELF-STUDY COURSES AND OTHER FORMS OF PROFESSIONAL DEVELOPMENT. They have learned from experience that any person who has the ambition to give up a part of his or her spare time, or to use slack time at work, for professional development, has those qualities which make for leadership. This recognition is not a charitable gesture. It is sound business judgment upon the part of the employers.

FUEL THAT DRIVE

There is one weakness in people for which there is no remedy. It is the universal weakness of LACK OF AMBITION! People, especially those on salary, who schedule their spare time and slack time to provide for self-improvement seldom remain at the bottom very long. Their action opens the way for the upward climb, removes many obstacles from their path, and gains the friendly interest of those who have the power to put them in the way of OPPORTUNITY.

The self-improvement or 'home study' method of training is especially suited to the needs of employed people who find, after leaving school, that they must acquire additional specialized knowledge, but cannot spare the time to go back to school.

The changed economic conditions that now prevail have made it necessary for thousands of people to find additional or new sources of income. For the majority of these, the solution to their problem may be found only by acquiring specialized knowledge. Many will be forced to change their occupation entirely. When merchants find that a certain line of merchandise is not selling, they usually supplant it with another that is in demand. The person whose business is that of marketing personal services must also be an efficient merchant. If the services do not bring adequate returns in one occupation, the individual must change to another, where broader opportunities are available.

Stuart Austin Wier prepared himself as a construction engineer and followed this line of work until the Depression limited his market to where it did not give him the income he required. He took inventory of himself, decided to change his profession to law, went back to school and took special courses by which he prepared himself as a corporation lawyer. Despite the fact the Depression had not ended, he completed his training, passed the bar examination, and quickly built a lucrative law practice in Dallas, Texas. He actually had to turn away clients.

Just to keep the record straight and to anticipate the alibis of those who will say, 'I couldn't go to school because I have a family to support' or 'I'm too old', I will add that Mr Wier was past 40 and married when he went back to school. Moreover, by carefully selecting highly specialized courses, in colleges best prepared to teach the subjects chosen, Mr Wier completed in two years the work for which the majority of law students require four years. IT PAYS TO KNOW HOW TO PURCHASE KNOWLEDGE!

The person who stops studying merely because he or she has finished school is forever hopelessly doomed to mediocrity, no matter what that person's calling. The way of success is the way of *continuous pursuit of knowledge*.

POINTS TO REMEMBER

1. Knowledge alone will not attract money unless it is systematically directed.
2. You can be ignorant despite completing the highest levels of education.
3. How to overpower your inferiority complexes.

5

APPLIED FAITH

If you had a definite major purpose, knew exactly what you wanted to do, had a mastermind alliance of people that could help you do it, and then had the sufficient faith to keep you going while you did it, that would be about all you would need.

Why do you suppose we need the fourteen additional principles? We need fourteen additional principles to induce you to make use of these three.

You need personal initiative. You need imagination. You need enthusiasm. In other words, this philosophy is like baking a cake. When you bake a cake, you don't put in just one ingredient. You put in a pinch of this, a pinch of that, a dash of the other thing, and then you put it in the stove and bake it. If you took out any one of those ingredients, you wouldn't end up with the same kind of cake. It's the same way with this philosophy. You can't leave out any one of these seventeen principles. It would be like taking a link out of a chain. You wouldn't have a chain anymore, you'd have two parts of a chain, but not a whole chain. The other fourteen principles are supporting principles of these three.

Faith is a state of mind that has been called the mainspring of the soul, to which one's aims, desires, plans and purposes may be translated into their physical or financial equivalent.

There are the fundamentals of faith, but by applied faith, I'm talking about something vastly different from mere belief. The word *applied* means what? Action. It's the action part of faith. Without action, faith is nothing but just daydreaming. There are a lot of people who believe in things but don't do anything about them, engaging only in daydreaming. Applied faith is an active faith.

FAITH AND THE FIRST THREE PRINCIPLES OF SUCCESS

1. Definiteness of Purpose. Purpose is supported by a personal initiative and action, action, action—the more action, the better. That means continual action, not only on your part but also on the part of those that may be cooperating with you or your mastermind allies.

2. Positive Mental Attitude. A positive mind, free from all negatives such as fear, envy, hatred, jealousy, and greed, is essential. Mental attitude determines the effectiveness of faith. It's a fact. The frame of mind that you are in when you pray will determine what happens as a result of that prayer. There's no two ways about it. You can test it for yourself and find out.

I have no doubt that you have had the experiences that I've had, sending out prayers that didn't produce anything but a negative result. Do you suppose there is anybody that *didn't* have that experience at one time or another? When you pray, unless you have such absolute faith that whatever you are going after you're going to acquire, and that you can see it in advance in your possession before you start asking for it, chances are the effect of your prayer is going to be negative.

3. Mastermind Alliance. A mastermind alliance convenes one or more other people who radiate courage based on faith and are suited mentally and spiritually to one's needs in carrying out a given purpose.

ELEMENTS OF APPLIED FAITH

1. Every adversity carries with it the seed of an equivalent benefit; temporary defeat is not failure until it has been accepted as such. Do you know where the majority of people fall down in connection with their application of their faith? It's when they're defeated and they accept that defeat as being something they can't do anything about. Instead of beginning immediately to search for that seed of an equivalent benefit that's in *every* defeat, they become moody and broody, discouraged, and build up inferiority complexes. Instead, they could reverse the order and *use* defeat as nothing more than a temporary point from which to make another effort.

My saying that every adversity carries with it the seed of an equivalent benefit, that every defeat and every failure carries the seed of an equivalent benefit, wouldn't mean anything to you unless I made application of it, and gave you illustration after illustration. If you examine enough illustrations in your own experience, you'll see that it always works out that way. That's why I want you to look closely at the adversities that come to you.

Do you know that your adversities are often your greatest blessings? Do you know the greatest blessing that ever came into my life? Of course, it was the loss of my mother.

Ordinarily, the greatest catastrophe that could overtake a child would be to lose his mother at the age of nine years.

Why do I say that was the greatest, greatest blessing? Because it brought me a new mother to take her place, one who is responsible for everything that I've achieved and everything that I shall achieve. Without her influence, I'd still be fighting rattlesnakes, drinking mountain liquor and fighting feuds. My relatives are still doing that same thing, so there's no reason to expect that I wouldn't be. I've had a lot of other adversities, and I want to tell you that without some twenty major adversities I've gone through, I would never have been able to pursue the soundness of this philosophy—that there is a seed of equivalent benefit in every adversity.

Can you imagine any worse adversity to a man than to be informed that his son was born without any signs of ears and would be a deaf and dumb mute all of his life? Can you imagine anything worse than that? I'll always be thankful that because of my contact with Infinite Intelligence, my deaf son was provided with a sort of hearing system that gave him 65 per cent of his normal hearing and eventually 100 per cent with a modern hearing aid. He learned to live a normal life and I got the greatest demonstration of my entire experience in the power of faith. I couldn't have gotten it any other way. I couldn't have gotten it second-hand, I had to get it firsthand.

I never accepted that affliction of that child, not even before I saw him, and not even after I saw him. I never accepted it. His relatives accepted it. They wanted to put him in the school of underprivileged where he'd learn sign language and lip reading. I didn't even want him to know there *were* such things. When he was old enough to go to school, I had a fight with the school authorities every year just as regular as a clock, because they wanted to send him to a school for underprivileged children, to mix with the other children and see their afflictions. I didn't want him to know there were such things. I taught him from the very beginning that his not having any ears was a great blessing —and he believed it. Compassion led people to do things for him they wouldn't have done otherwise. He got a job as a salesman for the *Saturday Evening Post* and he led every salesman throughout the United States. He'd often go out with five dollars' worth of merchandise and come back with ten dollars in cash. He did that many times. People would look at him and say, 'Why that poor little fellow with no ears is out selling papers. I guess his parents are poor.' They'd give him a dollar bill and when he'd try to give them their change, they'd say, 'Oh, sonny, you just keep that.' So he'd often get a dollar apiece for the *Saturday Evening Post*. Not at all conscious today of any affliction, he's living a perfectly normal life because I taught him that an affliction, *any kind of an affliction*, can be transmuted into a benefit.

2. Applied faith requires the habit of affirming one's definite major purpose in the form of a prayer at least once daily. The subconscious mind only knows what you tell it, or what you allow other people to tell it, or what you allow the circumstances of life to tell it. It doesn't know the difference between a lie and the truth. It doesn't know the difference between a penny and a million dollars. It accepts the things that you send over, and if you send over predominating thoughts on poverty and ill health and failure, that's exactly what'll you get. No matter how much faith that you may have later on, you'll find out the subconscious responds to the mental attitude that you're maintaining during the day. It's necessary for you to affirm over and over again the objects that you are going to attain in life until you educate your subconscious mind to automatically attract to you the things that are related to what you're aiming to attain in life. You'll find that your mind is like an electrode magnet and once you charge it with a clear picture of what you want, it'll attract to you from the highways and the byways the things that you need to carry out that purpose.

3. Recognition of the existence of an Infinite Intelligence that gives order to the vast, entire universe. You are a minute expression of this intelligence and as such your mind has no limitation except those accepted or set up in your own mind. Let me repeat that statement. Your mind has no limitations whatsoever, except those that you allow to be established there or that you deliberately set up in your mind or accept. That's a pretty broad statement. However, the achievements of men like Mr Edison, Mr Ford, Mr Carnegie and Napoleon Hill (if you please) definitely support the idea that there is no limitation except that which you set up in your mind.

If I had ever wavered for one second in my belief of what I would do, from the time that I started with Mr Carnegie up until the time I gave this philosophy to the world, I would never have done it. How did I do it? Do you have any idea what played the strongest part in what I've achieved? It wasn't my brilliancy and it wasn't my outstanding intelligence. I have no more brilliance than the average person and no more intelligence than the average person. But, I believed that I could do it and I never stopped believing it. The harder the going was, the more I believed I would do it. If you can take that attitude toward yourself, throwing yourself over on the side of yourself when you're overtaken by adversity, or when people are against you, and not go *against* yourself, then you're using applied faith.

You've got to do that.

Do you know there are testing times for people? Nobody is permitted to attain a high state in life and stay there without being tested. Nobody is allowed to go into a well-managed business or go to a high position and stay there without being tested at lower positions until, step-by-step, he earns the right to be up on the top. I don't know how the Creator runs his business entirely, but I can catch a pretty good idea of how he does it from observing that part which I can understand. Of course, there's much more that I *can't* understand, but I can definitely see that he allows nobody to attain to a higher stage of life without giving him severe testing.

One of the most outstanding things that I found in my research was that the men of great achievement in all walks of life, and throughout the ages, were great only in proportion as they had been defeated and as they met with opposition. What an outstanding thing. It couldn't be a coincidence that every one of these outstanding men was exactly great in proportion as he had been small and as he had been opposed and as he had had to struggle.

I used to tell of my early struggles and tell some of my defeats. My business manager said it wasn't a good idea. I think it's a fine idea, because if you knew the amount of the major defeats that I have met, recognizing how I still kept my head above water and still live to deliver this philosophy, you'd say, 'If Hill can do it, I can do it too.' That's the only reason I ever spoke of it.

I don't mind what terms you use: God, Jehovah, Buddha or Muhammad. You can call it anything you want to. No matter what you call it, we're all talking about one first cause. There aren't two first causes, there's only one. There couldn't be two. There's one first cause that's responsible for this great universe we're living in—for you and for me and for everything that's in the universe. I call it Infinite Intelligence because I have students of all faiths and all religions all over the world and Infinite Intelligence happens to be a neutral term nobody can object to.

But unless you not only believe in that, unless you can prove to yourself, and absolutely put down on paper evidence that there is first cause that you can draw upon, you're not going to be able to make the fullest use of a definite plan.

One of my students asked me about my concept of Infinite Intelligence and if I meant the same thing as God. I said, 'Yes I do.' 'Well,' he said, 'can you prove the existence of your concept of God?' I replied, 'Everything in the universe is the finest evidence of Its existence, because of the orderliness of the universe.' Everything's orderly, from the electrons and protons in the smallest part of the matter, up to the largest suns that float through the heavens. Everything's in orderliness: no chaos, no running together of the planets. There's more evidence of a first cause than there is of anything that I know of. And, if you don't believe that, if you don't accept it, if you don't see it, if you don't feel it, and if you don't know it, then you won't know that you are a minute part of that Infinite Intelligence being expressed through your brain. If you recognize that, then you recognize the truth of what I said—that your only limitations are those which you set up in your mind, or permit somebody to set up there, or let circumstances establish there for you.

Careful inventory of your past defeats (and adversities from it) shows that all such experiences do carry the seed of an equivalent benefit.

POINTS TO REMEMBER

1. Without action, faith is nothing but just daydreaming.
2. Any kind of an affliction can be transmuted into a benefit.
3. You'll find that your mind is like an electrode magnet and once you charge it with a clear picture of what you want, it'll attract to you the things that you need.

6

ENTHUSIASM

Enthusiasm is a state of mind that inspires and arouses one to put *action* into the task at hand. It does more than this—it is contagious, and vitally affects not only the enthusiast, but all with whom he comes in contact.

Enthusiasm bears the same relationship to a human being that steam does to the locomotive—it is the vital moving force that impels *action*. The greatest leaders of men are those who know how to inspire enthusiasm in their followers. Enthusiasm is the most important factor entering into salesmanship. It is, by far, the most vital factor that enters into public speaking.

If you wish to understand the difference between a man who is enthusiastic and one who is not, compare Billy Sunday with the average man of his profession. The finest sermon ever delivered would fall upon deaf ears if it were not backed with enthusiasm by the speaker.

HOW ENTHUSIASM WILL AFFECT YOU

Mix enthusiasm with your work and it will not seem hard or monotonous. Enthusiasm will so energize your entire body that you can get along with less than half the usual amount of sleep and at the same time it will enable you to perform from two to three times as much work as you usually perform in a given period, without fatigue.

For many years I have done most of my writing at night. One night, while I was enthusiastically at work over my typewriter, I looked out of the window of my study, just across the square from the Metropolitan tower, in New York City, and saw what seemed to be the most peculiar reflection of the moon on the tower. It was of a silvery grey shade, such as I had never seen before. Upon closer inspection I found that the reflection was that of the early morning sun and not that of the moon. It was daylight! I had been at work all night, but I was so engrossed in my work that the night had passed as though it were but an hour. I worked at my task all that day and all the following night without stopping, except for a small amount of light food.

Two nights and one day without sleep, and with but little food, without the slightest evidence of fatigue, would not have been possible had I not kept my body energized with *enthusiasm* over the work at hand.

Enthusiasm is not merely a figure of speech; it is a vital force that you can harness and use with profit.

Without it you would resemble an electric battery without electricity.

Enthusiasm is the vital force with which you recharge your body and develop a dynamic personality. Some people are blessed with natural *enthusiasm*, while others must acquire it. The procedure through which it may be developed is simple. It begins by the doing of the work or rendering of the service which one likes best. If you should be so situated that you cannot conveniently engage in the work which you like best, for the time being, then you can proceed along another line very effectively by adopting a *definite chief aim* that contemplates your engaging in that particular work at some future time.

Lack of capital and many other circumstances over which you have no immediate control may force you to engage in work which you do not like, but no one can stop you from determining in your own mind what your *definite chief aim* in life shall be, nor can anyone stop you from planning ways and means for translating this aim into reality, nor can anyone stop you from mixing *enthusiasm* with your plans.

Happiness, the final object of all human effort, is a state of mind that can be maintained only through the hope of future achievement. Happiness lies always in the future and never in the past. The happy person is the one who dreams of heights of achievement that are yet unattained. The home you intend to own, the money you intend to earn and place in the bank, the trip you intend to take when you can afford it, the Position in life you intend to fill when you have prepared yourself, and the preparation, itself—these are the things that produce happiness. Likewise, these are the materials out of which your *definite chief aim* is formed; these are the things over which you may become *enthusiastic*, no matter what your present station in life may be.

More than twenty years ago I became enthusiastic over an idea. When the idea first took form in my mind I was unprepared to take even the first step toward its transformation into reality. But I nursed it in my mind—I became *enthusiastic* over it as I looked ahead, in my imagination, and saw the time when I would be prepared to make it a reality.

The idea was this: I wanted to become the editor of a magazine, based upon the Golden Rule, through which I could inspire people to keep up courage and deal with one another squarely.

Finally my chance came! On armistice day, 1918, I wrote the first editorial for what was to become the material realization of a hope that had lain dormant in my mind for nearly a score of years.

With *enthusiasm* I poured into that editorial the emotions which I had been developing in my heart over a period of more than twenty years. My dream had come true. My editorship of a national magazine had become a reality.

As I have stated, this editorial was written with *enthusiasm*. I took it to a man of my acquaintance and with *enthusiasm* I read it to him. The editorial ended in these words, 'At last my twenty-year- old dream is about to come true. It takes money, and a lot of it, to publish a national magazine, and I haven't the slightest idea where I am going to get this essential factor, but this is worrying me not at all because *I know I am going to get it somewhere!*' As I wrote those lines, I mixed *enthusiasm* and faith with them.

I had hardly finished reading this editorial when the man to whom I read it—the first and only person to whom I had shown it—said, 'I can tell you where you are going to get the money, for I am going to supply it.' And he did!

Yes, *enthusiasm* is a vital force; so vital, in fact, that no man who has it highly developed can begin even to approximate his power of achievement.

Before passing to the next step in this lesson, I wish to repeat and to emphasize the fact that you may develop *enthusiasm* over your *definite chief aim* in life, no matter whether you are in position to achieve that purpose at this time or not. You may be a long way from realization of your *definite chief aim,* but if you will kindle the fire of *enthusiasm* in your heart, and keep it burning, before very long the obstacles that now stand in the way of your attainment of that purpose will melt away as if by the force of magic, and you will find yourself in possession of power that you did not know you possessed.

HOW YOUR ENTHUSIASM WILL AFFECT OTHERS

We come, now, to the discussion of one of the most important subjects of this Reading Course, namely, *suggestion.*

In the preceding lessons we have discussed the subject of *auto-suggestion,* which is self-suggestion.

Suggestion is the principle through which your words and your acts and even *your state of mind* influence others. If you now understand and accept the principle of telepathy (the communication of thought from one mind to another without the aid of signs, symbols or sounds) as a reality, you of course understand why *enthusiasm* is contagious, and why it influences all within its radius.

When your own mind is vibrating at a high rate, because it has been stimulated with *enthusiasm,* that vibration registers in the minds of all within its radius, and especially in the minds of those with whom you come in close contact. When a public speaker 'senses' the feeling that his audience is 'en rapport' (in harmony) with him he merely recognizes the fact that his own *enthusiasm* has influenced the minds of his listeners until their minds are vibrating in harmony with his own.

When the salesman 'senses' the fact that the 'psychological' moment for closing a sale has arrived, he merely feels the effect of his own *enthusiasm* as it influences the mind of his prospective buyer and places that mind 'en rapport' with his own.

The subject of *suggestion* constitutes so vitally an important part of this lesson, and of this entire course, that I will now proceed to describe the three mediums through which it usually operates; namely, what you say, what you do and what you *think!*

When you are enthusiastic over the goods you are selling or the services you are offering, or the speech you are delivering, your state of mind becomes obvious to all who hear you, *by the tone of your voice.*

Whether you have ever thought of it in this way or not, it is the tone in which you make a statement, more than it is the statement itself, that carries conviction or fails to convince. No mere combination of words can ever take the place of a deep belief in a statement that is expressed with burning *enthusiasm.* Words are but devitalized sounds unless coloured with feeling that is born of *enthusiasm.*

Here the printed word fails me, for I can never express with mere type and paper the difference between words that fall from unemotional lips, without the fire of *enthusiasm* hack of them, and those which seem to pour forth from a heart that is bursting with eagerness for expression. The difference is there, however.

Thus, *what you say*, and the way in which you say it, conveys a meaning that may be just the opposite to what is intended. This accounts for many a failure by the salesman who presents his arguments in words which seem logical enough, but lack the colouring that can come only from *enthusiasm* that is born of sincerity and belief in the goods he is trying to sell. His, words said one thing, but the tone of his voice *suggested* something entirely different; therefore, no sale was made.

That which you *say* is an important factor in the operation of the principle of *suggestion,* but not nearly so important as that which you *do. Your acts will count for more than your words,* and woe unto you if the two fail to harmonize.

If a man preach the Golden Rule as a sound rule of conduct his words will fall upon deaf ears if he does not practice that which he preaches. The most effective sermon that any man can preach on the soundness of the Golden Rule is that which he preaches, by *suggestion,* when he applies this rule in his relationships with his fellow men.

If a salesman of Ford automobiles drives up to his prospective purchaser in a Buick, or some other make of car, all the arguments he can present in behalf of the Ford will be without effect.

Once I went into one of the offices of the Dictaphone Company to look at a Dictaphone (dictating machine). The salesman in charge presented a logical argument as to the machine's merits, while the stenographer at his side was transcribing letters from a shorthand notebook. His arguments in favour of a dictating machine, as compared with the old method of dictating to a stenographer, did not impress me, because his actions were not in harmony with his words.

Your *thoughts* constitute the most important of the three ways in which you apply the principle of *suggestion*, for the reason that they control the tone of your words and, to some extent at least, your actions. If your *thoughts* and your *actions* and your *words* harmonize, you are bound to influence those with whom you come in contact, more or less toward your way of thinking.

We will now proceed to analyse the subject of *suggestion* and to show you exactly how to apply the principle upon which it operates. As we have already seen, *suggestion* differs from auto-suggestion only in one way—we use it, consciously or unconsciously, when we influence others, while we use *auto-suggestion* as a means of influencing ourselves.

Before you can influence another person through *suggestion*, that person's mind must be in a state of neutrality; that is, it must be open and receptive to your method of *suggestion*. Right here is where most salesmen fail—they try to make a sale before the mind of the prospective buyer has been rendered receptive or neutralized. This is such a vital point in this lesson that I feel impelled to dwell upon it until there can be no doubt that you understand the principle that I am describing.

When I say that the salesman must neutralize the mind of his prospective purchaser before a sale can be made I mean that the prospective purchaser's mind must be credulous. A state of confidence must have been established and it is obvious that there can be no set rule for either establishing confidence or neutralizing the mind to a state of openness. Here the ingenuity of the salesman must supply that which cannot be set down as a hard and fast rule.

I know a life insurance salesman who sells nothing but large policies, amounting to $100,000 and upward. Before this man even approaches the subject of insurance with a prospective client he familiarizes himself with the prospective client's complete history, including his education, his financial status, his eccentricities if he has any, his religious preferences and other data too numerous to be listed. Armed with this information, he manages to secure an introduction under conditions which permit him to know the Prospective client in a social as well as a business way. Nothing is said about the sale of life insurance during his first visit, nor his second, and sometimes he does not approach the subject of insurance until he has become very well acquainted with the prospective client.

All this time, however, he is not dissipating his efforts. He is taking advantage of these friendly visits for the purpose of neutralizing his prospective client's mind; that is, he is building up a relationship of confidence so that when the time comes for him to talk life insurance that which he says will fall upon ears that *willingly listen.*

Some years ago I wrote a book entitled *How to Sell Your Services.* Just before the manuscript went to the publisher, it occurred to me to request some of the well-known men of the

United States to write letters of endorsement to be published in the book. The printer was then waiting for the manuscript; therefore, I hurriedly wrote a letter to some eight or ten men, in which I briefly outlined exactly what I wanted, but the letter brought back no replies. I had failed to observe two important prerequisites for success—I had written the letter so hurriedly that I had failed to inject the spirit of *enthusiasm* into it, and, I had neglected so to word the letter that it had the effect of neutralizing the minds of those to whom it was sent; therefore, I had not paved the way for the application of the principle of *suggestion.*

After I discovered my mistake, I then wrote a letter that was based upon strict application of the principle of *suggestion*, and this letter not only brought back replies from all to whom it was sent, but many of the replies were masterpieces and served, far beyond my fondest hopes, as valuable supplements to the book.

◆

NOT ALL ADVICE IS GOOD ADVICE

Suggestion is one of the most subtle and powerful principles of psychology. You are making use of it in all that you do and say and think, but, unless you understand the difference between negative suggestion and positive suggestion, you may be using it in such a way that it is bringing you defeat instead of success.

Science has established the fact that through the negative use of suggestion life may be extinguished. Some years ago, in France, a criminal was condemned to death, but before the time for his execution an experiment was performed on him which conclusively proved that through the principle of suggestion death, could be produced. The criminal was brought to the guillotine and his head was placed under the knife, after he had been blindfolded. A heavy, sharp edged plank was then dropped on his neck, producing a shock similar to that of a sharp edged knife. Warm water was then gently poured on his neck and allowed to trickle slowly down his spine, to imitate the flow of warm blood. In seven minutes the doctors pronounced the man dead. His imagination, through the principle of suggestion, had actually turned the sharp edged plank into a guillotine blade and stopped his heart from beating.

In the little town where I was raised, there lived an old lady who constantly complained that she feared death from cancer. During her childhood she had seen a woman who had cancer and the sight had so impressed itself upon her mind that she began to look for the symptoms of cancer in her own body. She was sure that every little ache and pain was the beginning of her long- looked-for symptom of cancer. I have seen her place her hand on her breast and have heard her exclaim, 'Oh, I am sure 1 have a cancer growing here. I can feel it.' When complaining of this imaginary disease, she always placed her hand on her left breast, where she believed the cancer was attacking her.

For more than twenty years she kept this up.

A few weeks ago she died—*with cancer on her left breast!* If suggestion will actually turn the edge of a plank into a guillotine blade and transform healthy body cells into parasites out of which cancer will develop, can you not imagine what it will do in destroying disease germs, if properly directed? *Suggestion* is the law through which mental healers work what appear to be miracles. I have personally witnessed the removal of parasitical growths known as warts, through the aid of suggestion, within forty-eight hours.

You—the reader of this lesson—can be sent to bed with *imaginary* sickness of the worst sort, in two hours' time or less, through the use of *suggestion*. If you should start down the street and three or four people in whom you had confidence should meet you and each exclaim that you look ill you would be ready for a doctor.

I wish to take advantage of this appropriate opportunity to state that all of the really big men whom I have had the pleasure of knowing have been the most willing and courteous men of my acquaintance when it came to rendering service that was of benefit to others. Perhaps that was one reason why they were *really* big men.

The human mind is a marvellous piece of machinery!

One of its outstanding characteristics is noticed in the fact that all impressions which reach it, either through outside *suggestion* or auto-suggestion, are recorded together in groups which harmonize in nature. The negative impressions are stored away, all in one portion of the brain, while the positive impressions are stored in another portion. When one of these impressions (or past experiences) is called into the conscious mind, through the principle of memory, there is a tendency to recall with it all others of a similar nature, just as the raising of one link of a chain brings up other links with it. For example, anything that causes a feeling of doubt to arise in a person's mind is sufficient to call forth all of his experiences which caused him to become doubtful. If a man is asked by a stranger to cash a check, immediately he remembers having cashed checks that were not good, or of having heard of others who did so. Through the law of association all similar emotions, experiences and sense impressions that reach the mind are filed away together, so that the recalling of one has a tendency to bring back to memory all the others.

To arouse a feeling of distrust in a person's mind has a tendency to bring to the surface every doubt-building experience that person ever had. For this reason successful salesmen endeavour to keep away from the discussion of subjects that may arouse the buyer's 'chain of doubt impressions' which he has stored away by reason of previous experiences. The successful salesman quickly learns that 'knocking' a competitor or a competing article may result in bringing to the buyer's mind certain negative emotions growing out of previous experiences which may make it impossible for the salesman to 'neutralize' the buyer's mind.

This principle applies to and controls every sense impression that is lodged in the human mind. Take the feeling of fear, for example; the moment we permit a single emotion that is related to fear to reach the conscious mind, it calls with it all of its unsavoury relations. A feeling of courage cannot claim the attention of the conscious mind while a feeling of fear is there. One or the other must dominate. They make poor roommates because they do not harmonize in nature. Like attracts like. Every thought held in the conscious mind has a tendency to draw to it other thoughts of a similar nature. You see, therefore, that these feelings, thoughts and emotions growing out of past experiences, which claim the attention of the conscious mind, are backed by a regular army of supporting soldiers of a similar nature, that stand ready to aid them in their work.

Deliberately place in your own mind, through the principle of auto-suggestion, the ambition to succeed through the aid of a *definite chief aim,* and notice how quickly all of your latent or undeveloped ability in the nature of past experiences will become stimulated and aroused to action in your behalf. Plant in a boy's mind, through the principle of *suggestion,* the ambition to become a successful lawyer or doctor or engineer or business man or financier, and if you plant that suggestion deeply enough, and keep it there, by repetition, it will begin to move that boy toward the achievement of the object of that ambition.

If you would plant a *suggestion* 'deeply', mix it generously with *enthusiasm,* for enthusiasm is the fertilizer that will insure its rapid growth as well as its permanency.

When that kind-hearted old gentleman planted in my mind the suggestion that I was a 'bright boy' and that I could make my mark in the world if I would educate myself, it was not so much *what* he said, as it was the *way in which he said it* that made such a deep and lasting impression on my mind. It was the way in which he gripped my shoulders and the look of confidence in his eyes that drove his suggestion so deeply into my subconscious mind that it never gave me any peace until I commenced taking the steps that led to the fulfilment of the suggestion.

This is a point that I would stress with all the power at my command. *It is not so much what you say as it is the TONE and MANNER in which you say it that makes, a lasting impression.*

It naturally follows, therefore, that sincerity of purpose, honesty and earnestness must be placed back of all that one says if one would make a lasting and favourable impression.

Whatever you successfully sell to others you must first sell to *yourself.*

POINTS TO REMEMBER

1. Enthusiasm is the vital moving force that impels *action*.
2. Thoughts can be influenced through suggestion and auto-suggestion.
3. Happiness is the final object of all human effort.

7

LEARN TO SEE

When he was born, George W. Campbell was blind. 'Bilateral congenital cataracts,' the doctor called it.

George's father looked at the doctor, not wanting to believe. 'Isn't there anything you can do? Wouldn't an operation help?'

'No,' said the doctor. 'As of now, we know of no way to treat this condition.'

George Campbell couldn't see, but the love and faith of his parents made his life rich. As a very young boy, he did not know that he was missing anything.

And then, when George was six years old, something happened which he wasn't able to understand. One afternoon he was playing with another youngster. The other boy, forgetting that George was blind, tossed a ball to him. 'Look out! It'll hit you!'

The ball did hit George—and nothing in his life was quite the same after that. George was not hurt, but he was greatly puzzled. Later he asked his mother, 'How could Bill know what's going to happen to me before I know it?'

His mother sighed, for now the moment she dreaded had arrived. Now it was necessary for her to tell her son for the first time, 'You are blind.'

And here is how she did it, 'Sit down, George,' she said

softly as she reached over and took one of his hands. 'I may not be able to describe it to you, and you may not be able to understand, but let me try to explain it this way.' And sympathetically she took one of his little hands in hers and started counting the fingers.

'One—two—three—four—five. These fingers are similar to what is known as the five senses.' She touched each finger between her thumb and index finger in sequence as she continued the explanation.

'This little finger for hearing; this little finger for touch; this little finger for smell; this one for taste,' and then she hesitated before continuing, 'this little finger for sight. And each of the five senses, like each of the five fingers, sends messages to your brain.'

Then she closed the little finger which she had named 'sight' and tied it so that it would stay next to the palm of George's hand.

'George, you are different from other boys,' she explained, 'because you have the use of only four senses, like four fingers: one, hearing—two, touch—three, smell—and four, taste. But you don't have the use of your sense of sight. Now I want to show you something. Stand up,' she said gently.

George stood up. His mother picked up his ball. 'Now hold out your hand as if you were going to catch this,' she said.

George held out his hands, and in a moment he felt the hard ball hit his fingers. He closed them tightly around it and caught it.

'Fine. Fine,' said his mother. 'I never want you to forget what you have just done. You can catch a ball with four fingers instead of five, George. You can also *catch* and *hold* a full and happy life with four senses instead of five—if you get in there and keep trying.' Now George's mother had used a metaphor, and such a simple figure of speech is one of the quickest and most effective methods of communicating ideas between persons.

George never forgot the symbol of "'our fingers instead of five'. It meant to him the symbol of hope. And whenever he became discouraged because of his handicap, he used the symbol as a self-motivator. It became a form of self-suggestion to him. For he would repeat 'four fingers instead of five' frequently. At times of need it would flash from his subconscious to his conscious mind.

And he found that his mother was right. He was able to catch a full life, and hold it with the use of the four senses which he did have.

APPRECIATION FOR THE SENSE OF SIGHT

But George Campbell's story doesn't end here.

In the middle of his junior year at high school the boy became ill, and it was necessary for him to go to the hospital. While George was convalescing, his father brought him information from which he learned that science had developed a cure for congenital cataracts. Of course, there was a chance of failure but—the chances for success far outweighed those for failure.

George wanted so much to see that he was willing to risk failure in order to see.

During the next six months four delicate surgical operations were performed—two on each eye. For days George lay in the darkened hospital room with bandages over his eyes.

And finally the day came for the bandages to be removed. Slowly, carefully, the doctor unwound the gauze from around George's head and over his eyes. There was only a blur of light.

George Campbell was still technically blind!

For one awful moment he lay thinking. And then he heard the doctor moving beside his bed. Something was being placed over his eyes.

'Now, can you see?' came the doctor's question.

George raised his head slightly from the pillow. The blur of light became colour, the colour a form, a figure.

'George!' a voice said. He recognized the voice. It was his mother's voice.

For the first time in his 18 years of life George Campbell was seeing his mother. There were the tired eyes, the wrinkled, 62-year-old face, and the knotted and gnarled hands. But to George she was most beautiful.

To him—she was an angel. The years of toil and patience, the years of teaching and planning, the years of being his seeing eyes, the love and affection: that was what George saw.

To this day he treasures his first visual picture: the sight of his mother. And, as you will see, he learned an appreciation for his sense of sight from this first experience.

'None of us can understand,' he says, 'the miracle of sight, unless we have had to do without it.'

Seeing is a learned process. But George also learned something that is very helpful to anyone interested in the study of PMA. He will never forget the day he saw his mother standing before him in the hospital room, and did not know who she was—or even what she was—until he heard her speak. 'What we see,' George points out, 'is always an interpretation of the mind. We have to train the mind to interpret what we see.'

This observation is backed up by science. 'Most of the process of seeing is not done by the eyes at all,' says Dr Samuel Renshaw, in describing the mental process of seeing. 'The eyes act as hands which reach "out there" and grab meaningless "things" and bring them into the brain. The brain then turns the "things" over to the memory. It is not until the brain interprets in terms of comparative action that we really *see* anything.'

Some of us go through life 'seeing' very little of the power and the glory around us. We do not properly filter the information that our eyes give us through the mental processes of the brain. As a result we often behold things without really *seeing* them at all. We receive physical impressions without grasping their meaning to us. We do not, in other words, put PMA to work on the impressions that are sent to our brain.

Is it time to have your mental vision checked? Not your physical vision —that is a matter for the medical specialists. But mental vision, like physical vision, can become distorted. When it does you can grope in a haze of false concepts … bumping and hurting yourself and others unnecessarily.

The most common physical weaknesses of the eye are two opposite extremes—nearsightedness and farsightedness. These are the major distortions of mental vision, too.

The person who is mentally nearsighted is apt to overlook objects and possibilities that are distant. He pays attention only to the problems immediately at hand and is blind to the opportunities that could be his by thinking and planning in terms of the future. You are nearsighted if you do not make plans, form objectives and lay the foundation for the future.

On the other hand, the mentally farsighted person is apt to overlook possibilities that are right before him. He does not see the opportunities at hand. He sees only a dream-world of the future, unrelated to the present. He wants to start at the top rather than move up step by step—and he does not recognize that the only job where you can start at the top is the job of digging a hole.

They looked and recognized what they saw. So, in the

process of learning to see, you will want to develop both your near sight and your far sight. The advantages to the man who knows how to see what is directly in front of him are enormous. For years the people in the little town of Darby, Montana, used to look up at what they called Crystal Mountain. The mountain was given this name because erosion had exposed a ledge of a lightly sparkling crystal that looked something like rock salt. A pack trail was built directly across the outcropping as early as 1937. But it wasn't until the year 1951—14 years later—that anyone bothered to stoop down, pick up a piece of the sparkling material, and really look at it.

START SEEING MORE THAN WHAT YOU WANT TO SEE

It was in this year 1951 that two Darby men, Mr A. E. Cumley and Mr L. I. Thompson, saw a mineral collection displayed in the town. Thompson and Cumley became very excited. There in the mineral display were specimens of beryl which, according to the attached card, was used in atomic energy research. Immediately Thompson and Cumley staked claims on Crystal Mountain. Thompson sent a specimen of the ore to the Bureau of Mines office in Spokane, together with a request to send an examiner to see a 'very large deposit' of the mineral. Later that year the Bureau of Mines sent a bulldozer up the mountain and scraped off enough of the outcropping to determine that here indeed was one of the world's greatest deposits of extremely valuable beryllium. Today, heavy earth-moving trucks struggle up the mountain and work their way back down again, weighted down with the extremely heavy ore, while at the bottom, virtually waiting with dollar bills in their hands, are representatives of the United States Steel Company and the United States Government, each anxious to buy the highly valued ore. All because one day two young men not only observed with their eyes, but took the trouble to see with their minds. Today these men are well on their way to being multimillionaires.

A mentally farsighted person could not have done what Thompson and Cumley did—if his mental vision were distorted. For he is the man who can see only far-off values while the advantages that lie at his feet go unclaimed. Are there fortunes right at your doorstep? Look about you. As you go about your daily chores are there small areas of irritation? Perhaps you can think of a way to overcome them—a way that will be helpful not only to yourself but to others. Many a man has made a fortune by meeting such homely needs. This was so of the man who invented the bobby pin and the one who devised the paper clip. It was so of the man who invented the zipper, and the metal pants-fastener. Look about you. Learn to see. You may find *Acres of Diamonds* in your own backyard.

But mental nearsightedness can be just as much of a problem as mental farsightedness. The man with this problem sees only what is under his nose, while more distant possibilities go unclaimed. He is the man who does not understand the power of a plan. He does not understand the value of thinking time. He is so busy with the problems that immediately confront him that he does not free his mind to range into the distance, reaching for new opportunities, seeking trends, getting the big picture.

Being able to see into the future is one of the most spectacular accomplishments of the human brain. Down in the heart of the citrus belt in Florida there is a little town called Winter Haven. The surrounding country is farmland. Certainly it would be considered by most people as an area entirely unsuited for a large tourist attraction. It is isolated. It has no beach, no mountains, only mile after mile of gently rolling hills with little lakes and cypress swamps down in the valleys.

But to this region came a man who 'saw' these cypress swamps with an eye that others had not used. His name was Richard Pope. Dick Pope bought one of these old cypress swamps, put a fence around it, and has turned down offers of at least a million dollars for the world-famous Cypress Gardens.

Of course, it really wasn't as simple as that. All along the line Dick Pope had to 'see' opportunities in his situation.

For instance, there was the question of advertising. Pope knew that the only way he would be able to draw the public into such an isolated place was through a barrage of advertising. But ads cost money. So what Dick Pope did was quite simple. He went into the popular photography business. He set up a photo supply house at Cypress Gardens, sold his visitors film and then taught them how to take spectacular shots of the Garden. He hired skilled water skiers. He put them through intricate performances while over a loudspeaker he announced to the public exactly what camera settings they should use in order to catch the action. And then, of course, when these travellers went back home, the very best trip pictures were always of Cypress Gardens. They gave Dick Pope the very best kind of advertising there is—word-of-mouth recommendations, with pictures!

This is the kind of creative seeing that we all need to develop. We need to learn how to look at our world with fresh eyes— seeing the opportunities that lie all about us, but simultaneously looking into the future for the chances that are there.

Seeing is a learned skill. But like any skill it must be exercised.

See another person's abilities, capacities and viewpoint. We may think we recognize our own talents; yet in this respect we may be blind. Let's illustrate with an example of a teacher who needed to have her mental vision checked. She was both nearsighted and farsighted. For she could not see either the present or the future potential abilities and capacities of her students, or their points of view.

Now everyone—the great and the near great—had to have a starting point. They weren't born brilliant and successful. As a matter of fact, some of our greatest men were regarded as quite stupid at times during their lives. It was not until they grasped a positive mental attitude and learned to comprehend their capabilities and envision definite goals that they started their climbs to success. But there was one young man, in particular, whom his teachers thought 'a stupid, muddle-headed blockhead'.

The youngster sat and drew pictures on his slate. He looked about and listened to everybody else. He asked 'impossible questions' but refused to reveal what he knew, even under the threat of punishment. The children called him 'dunce', and he generally stood at the foot of his class.

And this boy was Thomas Alva Edison. You will be inspired when you read the life story of Thomas A. Edison. He attended primary school for a total period of less than three months. The teacher and his schoolmates told him that he was stupid. Yet, he became an educated man after an incident in his life prompted him to turn his talisman from NMA to PMA. He developed into a gifted person. He became a great inventor.

What was that incident? What happened to Edison that changed his whole attitude? He told his mother about hearing the teacher tell the inspector at school that he was 'addled' and it wouldn't be worthwhile to keep him in school any longer.

His mother marched off to school with him and told all within range of her voice that her son, Thomas Alva Edison, had more brains than the teacher or the inspector.

Edison called his mother the most enthusiastic champion a boy ever had. And from that day forward he was a changed boy. He said, 'She cast over me an influence which has lasted all my life. The good effects of her early training I can never lose. My mother was always kind, always sympathetic, and she never misunderstood or misjudged me.' His mother's belief in him caused him to view himself in an entirely different light. It caused him to turn his talisman to PMA and take a positive mental attitude regarding studying and learning. This attitude taught Edison to view things with deeper mental insight, that enabled him to comprehend and develop inventions which benefited mankind. Perhaps the teacher didn't see because the teacher wasn't genuinely interested in helping the boy. His mother was.

You have a tendency to see what you want to see.

START USING ALL SENSES TO SUCCEED

To hear does not necessarily imply attention or application. *To listen* always does. Throughout *Success Through a Positive Mental Attitude* I urge you to listen to the message. This means: *to see* how you can relate and assimilate the principle into your own life.

Perhaps you'd like to see how you can relate the principle of the following experience into your own life.

Dr Roy Plunkett, a DuPont chemist, made an experiment. He failed. When he opened the test tube after the experiment, he observed that it apparently contained nothing. He was curious. He asked himself, 'Why?' He didn't throw the tube away as others might have done under similar circumstances. Instead, he weighed the tube. And, to his surprise, it weighed more than a tube of like make and design. So, again, Dr Plunkett asked himself, 'Why?'

In searching for the answer to his questions, he discovered that marvellous transparent plastic, tetrafluoroethylene, commonly known as Teflon. During the Korean War, the United States government contracted for DuPont's entire output.

When there is something you don't understand, ask yourself, 'Why?' Look at it more closely. You may make a great discovery.

Ask yourself questions. Asking yourself or others questions about things that puzzle you may reward you richly. This very procedure led to one of the world's greatest scientific discoveries.

A young Englishman, while vacationing on his grandmother's farm, was relaxing. He was lying on his back under an apple tree and engaging in thinking time. An apple fell to the ground. This young man was a student of higher mathematics.

'Why does the apple fall to the ground?' he asked himself. 'Does the earth attract the apple? Does the apple attract the earth? Does each attract the other? What is the universal principle involved?'

Isaac Newton used his power to think and he made a discovery. To see mentally is to think. He found the answers he was looking for; the earth and the apple attracted each other, and the law of attraction of mass to mass applies to the entire universe.

Newton discovered the law of gravitation because he was observant and sought the answers to what he observed. Another man, because he exercised his powers of observation and acted upon what he perceived, found happiness and great wealth. Newton asked himself questions. The other man sought expert advice.

He became wealthy because he accepted advice. In Toba,

Japan, in the year 1869, when he was just eleven years old, Kokichi Mikimoto continued his father's business as the village noodle maker. His father had developed an illness that prevented him from working. The youngster supported his six brothers, three sisters and his parents. In addition to making the noodles daily, young Mikimoto had to sell them. He proved to be a good salesman.

Mikimoto had previously been tutored by a Samurai who taught, *'Exemplification of true faith consists of acts of kindness and love for one's fellowmen, not mere formal prayers uttered by rote.'*

And with this basic PMA philosophy of positive action, Mikimoto became a *doer*. He developed the habit of converting ideas into reality.

At the age of twenty he fell in love with the daughter of a Samurai. The young man knew that his future father-in-law would not bless his daughter's marriage with a noodle maker. Therefore, he was motivated to harmonize with this known power. He changed his occupation and became a pearl merchant.

Like many persons who achieve success in any part of the world, Mikimoto kept searching for specific knowledge that would help him in his new activity. He, like the great industrialists of our day, sought help from a university. Professor Yoshikichi Mizukuri told Mikimoto of a theory of one of the laws of nature that had never been proved.

The professor said, 'A pearl is formed in an oyster when a foreign object, like a grain of sand, is stuck in the oyster. If the foreign object does not kill the oyster, nature covers the object with the same secretion that forms the mother-of-pearl in the lining of the oyster's shell.'

Mikimoto was thrilled! He could hardly wait to get the answer to the question he asked himself, 'Can I raise pearls by deliberately planting a tiny foreign object in the oyster and letting nature take its course?'

He converted a theory into a positive action once he learned to see.

Mikimoto had been taught to see by that university professor. And then he used the power of his imagination. He engaged in creative thinking. He used deductive reasoning. He decided that if all pearls were formed only when a foreign object entered the oyster, he could develop pearls by using nature's laws. He could plant foreign objects in the oysters and force them to produce pearls. He learned to observe and act and he became a successful man.

Now a study of Mikimoto's life indicates that he employed all the seventeen success principles. For knowledge doesn't make you successful. But application of the knowledge will. *Action!*

Many of the ideas which come to us as we learn to see with fresh eyes will strike others as bold. These ideas can either frighten us or, if we act on them, make our fortunes. Here is another true story of pearls. This time the hero is a young American, Joseph Goldstone. He sold jewellery to Iowa farmers, door-to-door.

Then one day in the heart of the Depression he learned that the Japanese were producing beautiful cultured pearls. Here was quality, and it could be sold at a fraction of the cost of natural pearls!

Joe 'saw' a great opportunity. In spite of the fact that it was a Depression year, he and his wife, Esther, converted all their tangible assets into cash and set out for Tokyo. They landed in Japan with less than $1,000 —but they had their plan and lots of PMA.

They obtained an interview with Mr K. Kitamura, head of the Japanese Pearl Dealers Association. Joe was aiming high.

He told Mr Kitamura of his plan for merchandising Japanese cultured pearls in the United States, and asked Mr Kitamura for an initial credit of $100,000 in pearls. This was a fantastic sum, especially in a period of depression. After several days, however, Mr Kitamura agreed.

The pearls sold well. The Goldstones were well on their way to becoming wealthy. A few years later, they decided they wanted to establish their own pearl farm, which they did with the help of Mr Kitamura. Once again they 'saw' opportunity where others had seen nothing. Experience proved that the mortality rate of oysters into which a foreign object had been artificially inserted was over 50 per cent.

'How can we eliminate this great loss?' they asked themselves.

After much study, the Goldstones began to use on the oysters the methods employed in hospital rooms. The outside shells were scraped and scrubbed to reduce the danger of infection to the oyster. The 'surgeon' used a liquid anaesthetic that relaxed the oyster. Then he slipped a tiny clam pellet into each oyster as a nucleus for the pearl that was to be formed. The incision was made with a sterilized scalpel. Then the oyster was put into a cage, and the cage was dropped back into the water. Every four months cages were raised and the oysters were given a physical checkup. Through these techniques, 90 per cent of the oysters lived and developed pearls, and the Goldstones went on to acquire a fabulous fortune.

Time and again we see how men and women have become successful after they learned to apply mental perception. The ability to see is much more than the physical process of taking light rays through the retina of the eye. It is the skill of interpreting what you see and applying that interpretation to your life and the lives of others.

Learning to see will bring to you opportunities that you

never dreamed existed. However, there is more to success through PMA than learning mental perception. You must also learn to act on what you learn. Action is important because through action you get things done.

POINTS TO REMEMBER

1. Hope as a self-motivator.
2. What we see is always an interpretation of the mind.
3. Start seeing beyond what reaches the eye.

8

THE HABIT OF SAVING

To advise one to save money without describing how to save would be somewhat like drawing the picture of a horse and writing under it, 'This is a horse.' It is obvious to all that the saving of money is one of the essentials for success, but the big question uppermost in the minds of the majority of those who do not save is, 'How can I do it?'

The saving of money is solely a matter of *habit*. For this reason this lesson begins with a brief analysis of the Law of Habit.

It is literally true that man, through the Law of Habit, shapes his own personality. Through repetition, any act indulged in a few times becomes a habit, and the mind appears to be nothing more than a mass of motivating forces growing out of our daily habits.

When once fixed in the mind a habit voluntarily impels one to action. For example, follow a given route to your daily work, or to some other place that you frequently visit, and very soon the habit has been formed and your mind will lead you over that route without thought on your part. Moreover, if you start out with the intention of traveling in another direction, without keeping the thought of the change in routes constantly in mind, you will find yourself following the old route.

Public speakers have found that the telling over and over again of a story, which may be based upon pure fiction, brings into play the Law of Habit, and very soon they forget whether— the story is true or not.

WALLS OF LIMITATION BUILT THROUGII IIABIT

Millions of people go through life in poverty and want because they have made destructive use of the Law of Habit. Not understanding either the Law of Habit or the Law of Attraction through which 'like attracts like', those who remain in poverty seldom realize that they are where they are as the result of their own acts.

Fix in your mind the thought that your ability is limited to a given earning capacity and you will never earn more than that, because the Law of Habit will set up a definite limitation of the amount you can earn, your subconscious mind will accept this limitation, and very soon you will feel yourself 'slipping' until finally you will become so hedged in by FFAR OF POVERTY (one of the six basic fears) that opportunity will no longer knock at your door; your doom will be sealed; your fate fixed.

Formation of the Habit of Saving does not mean that you shall limit your earning capacity; it means just the opposite—that you shall apply this law so that it not only conserves that which you earn, in a systematic manner, but it also places you in the way of greater opportunity and gives you the vision, the self-confidence, the imagination, the enthusiasm, the initiative and leadership actually to increase your earning capacity.

'WE TALK AND THINK ONLY OF ABUNDANCE HERE. IF YOU HAVE A TALE OF WOE
PLEASE KEEP IT, AS WE DO NOT WANT IT.'

No business firm wants the services of a pessimist, and those who understand the Law of Attraction and the Law of Habit will no more tolerate the pessimist than they would permit a burglar to roam around their place of business, for the reason that one such person will destroy the usefulness of those around him.

In tens of thousands of homes the general topic of conversation is poverty and want, and that is just what they are getting. They think of poverty, they talk of poverty, they accept poverty as their lot in life. They reason that because their ancestors were poor before them they, also, must remain poor.

The poverty consciousness is formed as the result of the habit of thinking of and fearing poverty. 'Lo! the thing I had feared has come upon me.'

THE SLAVERY OF DEBT

Debt is a merciless master, a fatal enemy of the savings habit.

Poverty, alone, is sufficient to kill off ambition, destroy self-confidence and destroy hope, but add to it the burden of debt and all who are victims of these two cruel task-masters are practically doomed to failure.

No man can do his best work, no man can express himself in terms that command respect, no man can either create or carry out a definite purpose in life, with heavy debt hanging over his head. The man who is bound in the slavery of debt is just as helpless as the slave who is bound by ignorance, or by actual chains. The author has a very close friend whose income is $1,000 a month. His wife loves 'society' and tries to make a $20,000 showing on a $12,000 income, with the result that this poor fellow is usually about

$8,000 in debt. Every member of his family has the 'spending habit', having acquired this from the mother. The children, two girls and one boy, are now of the age when they are thinking of going to college, but this is impossible because of the father's debts. The result is dissension between the father and his children which makes the entire family unhappy and miserable.

It is a terrible thing even to think of going through life like a prisoner in chains, bound down and owned by somebody else on account of debts. The accumulation of debts is a habit. It starts in a small way and grows to enormous proportions slowly, step by step, until finally it takes charge of one's very soul.

Thousands of young men start their married lives with unnecessary debts hanging over their heads and never manage to get out from under the load. After the novelty of marriage begins to wear off (as it usually does) the married couple begin to feel the embarrassment of want, and this feeling grows until it leads, oftentimes, to open dissatisfaction with one another, and eventually to the divorce court.

A man who is bound by the slavery of debt has no time or inclination to set up or work out ideals, with the result that he drifts downward with time until he eventually begins to set up limitations in his own mind, and by these he hedges himself behind prison walls of FEAR and doubt from which he never escapes. No sacrifice is too great to avoid the misery of debt!

'Think of what you owe yourself and those who are dependent upon you and resolve to be no man's debtor,' is the advice of one very successful man whose early chances were destroyed by debt. This man came to himself soon enough to throw off the habit of buying that which he did not need and eventually worked his way out of slavery.

Most men who develop the habit of debt will not be so fortunate as to come to their senses in time to save themselves, because debt is something like quicksand in that it has a tendency to draw its victim deeper and deeper into the mire.

The Fear of Poverty is one of the most destructive of the six basic fears. The man who becomes hopelessly in debt is seized with this poverty fear, his ambition and self-confidence become paralysed, and he sinks gradually into oblivion.

There are two classes of debts, and these are so different in nature that they deserve to be here described, as follows:

1. There are debts incurred for luxuries which become a dead loss.
2. There are debts incurred in the course of professional or business trading which represent service or merchandise that can be converted back into assets.

The first class of debts is the one to be avoided. The second class may be indulged in, providing the one incurring the debts uses judgment and does not go beyond the bounds of reasonable limitation. The moment one buys beyond his limitations he enters the realm of speculation, and speculation swallows more of its victims than it enriches.

Practically all people who live beyond their means are tempted to speculate with the hope that they may recoup, at a single turn of the wheel of fortune, so to speak, their entire indebtedness. The wheel generally stops at the wrong place and, far from finding themselves out of debt, such people as indulge in speculation are bound more closely as slaves of debt.

The Fear of Poverty breaks down the willpower of its victims, and they then find themselves unable to restore their lost fortunes, and, what is still more sad, they lose all ambition to extricate themselves from, the slavery of debt.

Hardly a day passes that one may not see an account in the newspapers of at least one suicide as the result of worry over debts. The slavery of debt causes more suicides every year than all other causes combined, which is a slight indication of the cruelty of the poverty fear.

During the war millions of men faced the front-line trenches without flinching, knowing that death might overtake them any moment. Those same men, when facing the Fear of Poverty, often cringe and out of sheer desperation, which paralyses their reason, sometimes commit suicide.

The person who is free from debt may whip poverty and achieve outstanding financial success, but, if he is bound by debt, such achievement is but a remote possibility, and never a probability.

Fear of Poverty is a negative, destructive state of mind. Moreover, one negative state of mind has a tendency to attract other similar states of mind. For example, the Fear of Poverty may attract the fear of Ill Health, and these two may attract the fear of Old Age, so that the victim finds himself poverty-stricken, in ill health and actually growing old long before the time when he should begin to show the signs of old age. Millions of untimely, nameless graves have been filled by this cruel state of mind known as the Fear of Poverty!

Less than a dozen years ago a young man held a responsible position with the City National Bank, of New York City. Through living beyond his income he contracted a large amount of debts which caused him to worry until this destructive habit began to show up in his work and he was dismissed from the bank's service.

He secured another position, at less money, but his creditors embarrassed him so that he decided to resign and go away into another city, where he hoped to escape them until he had accumulated enough money to pay off his indebtedness. Creditors have a way of tracing debtors, so very soon they were close on the heels of this young man, whose employer found out about his indebtedness and dismissed him from his position.

He then searched in vain for employment for two months. One cold night he went to the top of one of the tall buildings on Broadway and jumped off. Debt had claimed another victim.

HOW TO MASTER THE FEAR OF POVERTY

To whip the Fear of Poverty one must take two very definite steps, providing one is in debt. First, quit the habit of buying on credit, and follow this by gradually paying off the debts that you have already incurred.

Being free from the worry of indebtedness you are ready to revamp the habits of your mind and redirect your course toward prosperity. Adopt, as a part of your Definite Chief Aim, the habit of saving a regular proportion of your income, even if this be no more than a penny a day. Very soon this habit will begin to lay hold of your mind and you will actually get joy out of saving.

Any habit may be discontinued by building in its place some other and more desirable habit. The 'spending' habit must be replaced by the 'saving' habit by all who attain financial independence.

Merely to discontinue an undesirable habit is not enough, as such habits have a tendency to reappear unless the place they formerly occupied in the mind is filled by some other habit of a different nature.

The discontinuance of a habit leaves a 'hole' in the mind, and this hole must be filled up with some other form of habit or the old one will return and claim its place.

Throughout this course many psychological formulas, which the student has been requested to memorize and practice, have been described. You will find such a formula in Lesson Three, the object of which is to develop Self-confidence.

These formulas may be assimilated so they become a part of your mental machinery, through the Law of Habit, if you will follow the instructions for their use which accompany each of them.

It is assumed that you are striving to attain financial independence. The accumulation of money is not difficult after you have once mastered the Fear of Poverty and developed in its place the Habit of Saving.

The author of this course would be greatly disappointed to know that any student of the course got the impression from anything in this or any of the other: lessons that success is measured by dollars alone.

However, money does represent an important factor in success, and it must be given its proper value in any philosophy intended to help people in becoming useful, happy and prosperous.

The cold, cruel, relentless truth is that in this age, of materialism a man is no more than so many grains of sand, which may be blown helter-skelter by every stray wind of circumstance, unless he is entrenched behind the power of money!

Genius may offer many rewards to those who possess it, but the fact still remains that genius without money with which to give it expression is but an empty, skeleton-like honour.

The man without money is at the mercy of the man who has it!

And this goes, regardless of the amount of ability he may possess, the training he has had or the native genius with which he was gifted by nature.

There is no escape from the fact that people will weigh you very largely in the light of bank balances, no matter who you are or what you can do. The first question that arises, in the minds of most people, when they meet a stranger, is, 'How much money has he?' If he has money he is welcomed into homes and business opportunities are thrown his way. All sorts of attention are lavished upon him. He is a prince, and as such is entitled to the best of the land.

But if his shoes arc run down at the heels, his clothes are not pressed, his collar is dirty and he shows plainly the signs of impoverished finances, woe be his lot, for the passing crowd will step on his toes and blow the smoke of disrespect in his face.

These are not pretty statements, but they have one virtue—THEY ARE TRUE!

This tendency to judge people by the money they have, or their power to control money, is not confined to any one class of people. We all have a touch of it, whether we recognize the fact or not.

Thomas A. Edison is one of the best known and most respected inventors in the world, yet it is no misstatement of facts to say that he would have remained a practically unknown, obscure personage had he not followed the habit of conserving his resources and shown his ability to save money.

Henry Ford never would have got to first base with his 'horseless carriage' had he not developed, quite early in life, the habit of saving. Moreover, had Mr Ford not conserved his resources and hedged himself behind their power he would have been 'swallowed up' by his competitors or those who covetously desired to take his business away from him, long, long years ago.

Many a man has gone a very long way toward success, only to stumble and fall, never again to rise, because of lack of money in times of emergency. The mortality rate in business each year, due to lack of reserve capital for emergencies, is stupendous. To this one cause are due more of the business failures than to all other causes combined!

Reserve Funds are essential in the successful operation of business!

Likewise, Savings Accounts are essential to success on the part of individuals. Without a savings fund the individual suffers in two ways: first, by inability to seize opportunities that come only to the person with some ready cash, and, second, by embarrassment due to some unexpected emergency calling for cash.

It might be said, also, that the individual suffers in still a third respect by not developing the Habit of Saving, through lack of certain other qualities essential for success which grow out of the practice of the Habit of Saving.

The nickels, dimes and pennies which the average person allows to slip through his fingers would, if systematically saved and properly put to work, eventually bring financial independence.

Through the courtesy of a prominent Building and Loan Association the following table has been compiled, showing what a monthly saving of $5.00, $10.00, $25.00 or $50.00 will amount to at the end of ten years. These figures are startling when one comes to consider the fact that the average person spends from $5.00 to $50.00 a month for useless merchandise or so-called 'entertainment'.

HOW MUCH SHOULD ONE SAVE?

The first question that will arise is, 'How much should one save?' The answer cannot be given in a few words, for the amount one should save depends upon many conditions, some of which may be within one's control and some of which may not be.

Generally speaking, a man who works for a salary should apportion his income about as follows:

Savings Account	20%
Living—Clothes, Food and Shelter	50%
Education	10%
Recreation	10%
Life Insurance	10%
	100%

The following, however, indicates the approximate distribution which the average man actually makes of his income:

Savings Account	*Nothing*
Living—Clothes, Food and Shelter	60%
Education	0%
Recreation	35%
Life Insurance	5%
	100%

Under the item of 'recreation' is included, of course, many expenditures that do not really 'recreate', such as money spent for alcoholic drinks, dinner parties and other similar items which may actually serve to undermine one's health and destroy character.

An experienced analyst of men has stated that he could tell very accurately, by examining a man's monthly budget, what sort of a life the man is living; moreover, that he will get most of his information from the one item of 'recreation'. This, then, is an item to be watched as carefully as the greenhouse keeper watches the thermometer which controls the life and death of his plants.

Those who keep budget accounts often include an item

called 'entertainment', which, in a majority of cases, turns out to be an evil because it depletes the income heavily and when carried to excess depletes, also, the health. We are living, right now, in an age when the item of 'entertainment' is altogether too high in most budget allowances. Tens of thousands of people who earn not more than $50.00 a week are spending as much as one third of their incomes for what they call 'entertainment', which comes in a bottle, with a questionable label on it, at anywhere from $6.00 to $12.00 a quart. Not only are these unwise people wasting the money that should go into a savings fund, but, of far greater danger, they are destroying both character and health.

Nothing in this lesson is intended as a preachment on morality, or on any other subject. We are here dealing with cold facts which, to a large extent, constitute the building materials out of which SUCCESS may be created.

However, this is an appropriate place to state some FACTS which have such a direct bearing on the subject of achieving success that they cannot be omitted without weakening this entire course in general and this lesson in particular.

We are all victims of HABIT!

Unfortunately for most of us, we are reared by parents who have no conception whatsoever of the psychology of habit, and, without being aware of their fault, most parents aid and abet their offspring in the development of the spending habit by overindulgence with spending money, and by lack of training in the Habit of Saving.

The habits of early childhood cling to us all through life.

Fortunate, indeed, is the child whose parents have the foresight and the understanding of the value, as a character builder, of the Habit of Saving, to inculcate this habit in the minds of their children.

It is a training that yields rich rewards.

Give the average man $100.00 that he did not contemplate receiving, and what will he do with it? Why, he will begin to cogitate in his own mind on how he can SPEND the money. Dozens of things that he needs, or THINKS he needs, will flash into his mind, but it is a rather safe bet that it will never occur to him (unless he has acquired the savings habit) to make this $100.00 the beginning of a savings account. Before night comes he will have the $100.00 spent, or at least he will have decided in his mind how he is going to SPEND IT, thus adding more fuel to the already too bright flame of Habit of Spending.

We are ruled by our habits!

It requires force of character, determination and power of firm DECISION to open a savings account and then add to it a regular, if small, portion of all subsequent income.

There is one rule by which any man may determine, well in advance, whether or not he will ever enjoy

the financial freedom and independence which is so universally desired by all men, and this rule has absolutely nothing to do with the amount of one's income.

The rule is that if a man follows the systematic habit of saving a definite proportion of all money he earns or receives in other ways, he is practically sure to place himself in a position of financial independence. If he saves nothing, he IS ABSOLUTELY SURE NEVER TO BE FINANCIALLY INDEPENDENT, no matter how much his income may be.

The one and only exception to this rule is that a man who does not save might possibly inherit such a large sum of money that he could not spend it, or he might inherit it under a trust which would protect it for him, but these eventualities are rather remote; so much so, in fact, that YOU cannot rely upon such a miracle happening to you.

POINTS TO REMEMBER

1. Mindset to make saving money a habit.
2. The poverty consciousness is formed as the result of the habit of thinking of and fearing poverty.
3. Beware of the merciless trap of debt.

9

THE SECRET OF GETTING THINGS DONE

In this chapter you will find the secret of getting things done. You will also receive a self-motivator so powerful that it will subconsciously force you to desirable action, for it is in reality a *self-starter*. Yet you can use it at will. When you do, you overcome procrastination and inertia.

If you do the things you don't want to do, or if you don't do the things that you do want to do, then this chapter is for you.

Those who achieve greatness employ this secret of getting things done. Take, for example, Maryknoll Father James Keller. Father Keller had been developing an idea for quite some time. He hoped to motivate 'little people to do big things by encouraging each to reach beyond his or her own little circle to the outside world.' The biblical command, "Go ye forth into all the world," was to him the symbol of an idea whereby the mission he had in mind could be fulfilled.

When he responded to this command, he employed the secret of getting things done. And when he did, he went into action. This happened in 1945. It was then that he organized the Christophers—an organization most unusual.

It has no chapters, no committees, no meetings, no dues. It

doesn't even have a membership in the usual sense of the word. It simply consists of people—no one can say how many—dedicated to an ideal. The Christophers operate on the concept that it is better for people to 'do something and pay nothing' than to 'pay dues and do nothing'. What is the ideal to which each is dedicated?

Each Christopher is dedicated to carry his religion with him wherever he goes throughout the day—into the dust and heat of the marketplace, into the highways and byways, into the home. And thus he brings the major truths of his faith to others.

The thrilling story is told by the Rev James Keller in *You Can Change the World*. It came about because he conceived and believed in an ideal. But he did little or nothing about it until he responded to the secret of getting things done.

You get the feel of this secret from the statement of E. E. Bauermeister, supervisor of education and correctional counsellor at the California Institution for Men, Chino, California, who told the me, 'I always tell the men in our self-adjustment class that too often what we read and profess becomes a part of our libraries and our vocabularies, instead of becoming a part of our lives.'

Remember the biblical statement: *for the good that I would, I do not; but the evil which I would not, that I do.* Now how can you train yourself to get into action immediately when it is desirable?

And then we told Mr Bauermeister how the good things we read and profess can become a part of our lives. We gave him the self-starter for getting things done.

How do you make the secret of getting things done a part of your life? By habit. And you develop habit through repetition. 'Sow an action and you reap a habit; sow a habit and you reap a character; sow a character and you reap a destiny,' said the great psychologist and philosopher William James. He was saying that you are what your habits make you. And you can choose your habits. You can develop any habit you wish when you use the self-starter.

Now what is the secret of getting things done and what is the self-starter that forces you to use this great secret?

The secret of getting things done is to act. The self-starter is the self-motivator, '*DO IT NOW!*'

As long as you live, never say to yourself, '*DO IT NOW!*' unless you follow through with desirable action. Whenever action is desirable and the symbol *DO IT NOW!* flashes from your subconscious mind to your conscious mind, immediately *act*.

Make it a practice to respond to the self-starter *DO IT NOW!* in little things. You will quickly develop the habit of a reflex response so powerful that in times of emergency or when opportunity presents itself, you will *act*.

Say you have a phone call that you should make but you have a tendency to procrastinate. And you have put off making that phone call. When the self-starter DO IT NOW! flashes from your subconscious to your conscious mind: *act*. Make that phone call immediately.

Or suppose, for example, that you set your alarm clock for 6:00 a.m. Yet when the alarm goes off, you feel sleepy, get up, turn off the alarm and go back to bed. You will have a tendency to develop a habit to do the same thing in the future. But if your subconscious mind flashes to the conscious DO IT NOW! then come what may—DO IT NOW! Stay up! Why? You want to develop the habit of responding to the self-starter DO IT NOW!

Now H. G. Wells learned the secret of getting things done. And H. G. Wells was a prolific writer because he did. He tried never to let a good idea slip away from him. While an idea was fresh, he immediately wrote down the thought that occurred to him. This would sometimes happen in the middle of the night. No matter. Wells would switch on the light, reach for the pencil and paper that were always beside his bed, and scribble away. And then he would drop off to sleep again.

Ideas that might have been forgotten were recalled when he refreshed his memory by looking at the flashes of inspiration that had been written down immediately when they occurred. This habit of Wells' was as natural and effortless to him as smiling is to you when a happy thought occurs.

ACT NOW AND PROCRASTINATE LATER

Many persons have the habit of procrastination. Because of it, they may miss a train, be late for work or even more important—miss an opportunity that could change the whole course of their lives for the better. History has recorded how battles have been lost because someone put off taking desirable action.

New students in our PMA Science of Success course sometimes state that the procrastination habit is the one they would like to eliminate. And then we reveal to them the secret of getting things done. We give them the self-starter. We may motivate them by telling them the true story of what the self-starter meant to a war prisoner in World War II.

What the self-starter meant to a war prisoner. Kenneth Erwin Harmon was a civilian employee for the Navy at Manila when the Japanese landed there. He was captured and held in a hotel for two days before he was sent to a prison camp.

On the first day, Kenneth saw that his roommate had a book under his pillow. 'May I borrow it?' he asked. The book was *Think and Grow Rich*. Kenneth began to read. As he read, he met the most important living person with the invisible talisman imprinted with PMA on one side and NMA on the reverse.

Before he started to read it, he had the feeling of despair. He fearfully looked ahead to possible torture—even death—in the prison camp. But now as he read his attitude became one inspired by hope. He had a craving to own the book. He wanted it with him during the dread days ahead. In discussing *Think and Grow Rich* with his fellow prisoner, he realized that the book meant a great deal to the owner.

'Let me copy it,' he said.

'Sure, go ahead,' was the response.

Kenneth Harmon employed the secret of getting things done. He swung into immediate action. In a fury of activity he began typing away. Word by word, page by page, chapter by chapter. Because he was obsessed with the possibility that it would be taken away at any moment, he was motivated to work night and day.

It was a good thing that he did for within an hour after the last page was completed, his captors led him away to the notorious Santo Tomas prison camp. He had finished in time because he started in time. Kenneth Harmon kept the manuscript with him during the three years and one month he was a prisoner. He read it again and again. And it gave him food for thought. It inspired him to: develop courage, make plans for the future and retain his mental and physical health. Many prisoners at Santo Tomas were permanently injured physically and mentally by malnutrition and fear—fear of the present and fear of the future. 'But I was better when I left Santo Tomas than when I was interned—better prepared for life—more mentally alert,' Kenneth Harmon told us. You get the *feel* of his thinking in his statement, 'Success must be continually practiced, or it will take wings and fly away.'

Now is the time to act.

For the secret of getting things done can change a person's attitude from negative to positive. A day that might have been ruined can become a pleasant day.

The day that might have been wasted. Jorgen Juhldahl, a student at the University of Copenhagen, worked one summer as a tourist guide. Because he cheerfully did much more than he was paid to do, some visitors from Chicago made arrangements for him to tour America. The itinerary included a day of sightseeing in Washington, D. C., while he was en route to Chicago.

On arriving in Washington, Jorgen checked in at the Willard Hotel, where his bill had been pre-paid. He was sitting on top of the world. In his coat pocket was his plane ticket to Chicago; in his hip pocket was his wallet with his passport and money. Then the young man was dealt a shocking blow!

While getting ready for bed, he found that his wallet and passport were missing. He ran downstairs to the hotel desk.

'We'll do everything we can,' said the manager.

But the next morning the wallet had still not been located. Jorgen Juhldahl had less than two dollars change in his pockets. Alone in a foreign country, he wondered what he should do. Wire his friends in Chicago and tell them what had happened? Go to the Danish embassy and report the lost passport? Sit at police headquarters until they had some news?

Then, all of a sudden, he said, 'No! I won't do any of these things! I'll see Washington. I may never be here again. I have one precious day in this great capital. After all, I still have my ticket to get me to Chicago tonight, and there'll be plenty of time then to solve the problem of the money and the passport.

But if I don't see Washington *now* I may never see it. I've walked miles at home, I'll enjoy walking here.

'Now is the time to be happy.

'I am the same man that I was yesterday before I lost my wallet. I was happy then. I should be happy now—just to be in America—just to have the privilege of enjoying a holiday in this great city.

'I won't waste my time in futile unhappiness over my loss.'

And so he headed off, on foot. He saw the White House and the Capitol, he visited the great museums, he climbed to the top of the Washington Monument. He wasn't able to take the tour of Arlington and some other places he'd wanted to see. But what he did see, he saw more thoroughly. He bought peanuts and candy and nibbled on them to keep from getting too hungry.

And when he got back to Denmark, the part of his American trip he remembered best was that day on foot in Washington—a day that might have gotten away from Jorgen Juhldahl if he had not employed the secret of getting things done. For he knew the truth in the statement. *NOW* is the time. He knew that *NOW* must be seized before it becomes: yesterday-I-could-have...

Incidentally, to round off his story, five days after that eventful day Washington police found both wallet and passport and sent them to him.

Are you scared of your own best ideas? One of the things that often prevents us from seizing the *NOW* is a certain timidity in the face of our own inspirations. We're a little bit afraid of our ideas when they first occur to us. They may seem novel or far-fetched. There's no doubt about it: it takes a certain boldness to step out on an untested idea. Yet it's exactly this kind of boldness that often produces the most spectacular results. The well-known writer, Elsie Lee, tells about Ruth Butler and her sister Eleanor, the daughters of a nationally known New York furrier.

'My father was a frustrated painter,' says Ruth. 'He had talent, but the need to earn a living left him no time to build a reputation as an artist. So he collected paintings. Later, he started buying paintings for Eleanor and me.' Thus, the girls developed a knowledge and appreciation of fine art, along with an impeccable sense of taste. As they grew older, friends would consult them on what types of paintings they should buy for their homes. Often they would loan pieces from their collection for brief periods.

One day Eleanor woke Ruth up at 3 a.m. 'Don't start arguing, but I have a *terrific* idea! We're going to form a Master Mind alliance.'

'Now what in the world is a Master Mind alliance?' Ruth asked.

'*A Master Mind alliance is coordination of knowledge and effort, in a spirit of harmony, between two or more people, for the attainment of a definite purpose.* And that's just what we're going to do. We're going into the business of renting paintings!'

And Ruth agreed. It *was* a terrific idea. They set to work the same day— although friends tried to warn them of dangers: their valued paintings might be lost or stolen; and there might be law suits and insurance problems. But they went right on working—accumulating $300 in capital and talking their father into loaning them the basement of his fur shop, rent free.

'We hauled 1,800 paintings from our own collections in among the coat forms,' Ruth recalls, 'and ignored Father's sad and disapproving eyes. The first year was grim—a real struggle.'

But the novel idea paid off. Their company, known as the New York Circulating Library of Paintings, became a success—

with about 500 paintings constantly on rental to business firms, doctors and lawyers and for use in homes. One valued client was an inmate of the Massachusetts Penitentiary for eight years. He wrote humbly that perhaps the Library wouldn't rent to him, considering his address. The paintings went to him rent free except for transportation costs. In return Ruth and Eleanor received a letter from prison authorities telling how the paintings were used in an art appreciation course that benefited many hundreds of prisoners. Ruth and Eleanor started their business with an idea. And then they backed their idea up with immediate action. The results were a profit to themselves and increased pleasure and happiness for many others.

CAN YOU DOUBLE YOUR INCOME IN 48 HOURS?

Are you ready to double your income? W. Clement Stone toured the Asiatic and Pacific areas as one of seven executives serving as representatives of the National Sales Executives International. On a Tuesday, Stone gave a talk on motivation to a group of businessmen at Melbourne, Australia. The following Thursday evening, he received a phone call. It was from Edwin H. East, manager of a firm that sold metal cabinets. Mr East was excited, 'Something wonderful has happened! You'll be as enthusiastic as I am when I tell you about it!'

'Tell me about it. What did happen?'

'An amazing thing! You gave your talk on motivation Tuesday. In your talk you recommended ten inspirational books. I bought *Think and Grow Rich* and started to read it that evening. I read for hours. The next morning I started reading it again and then I wrote on a piece of paper:

'My major definite aim is to double last year's sales this year. The amazing thing is: I did it in forty-eight hours.'

'How did you do it?' Mr Stone asked East. 'How did you double your income?'

East responded, 'In your speech on motivation, you told how Al Allen, one of your Wisconsin salesmen, tried to sell cold-canvass in a certain block. You said that Al was lucky because he worked all day and didn't make a sale.

'That evening, you said, Al Allen developed *inspirational dissatisfaction*. He determined that the following day he would again call on exactly the same prospects and sell more insurance policies that day than any of the other representatives in his group would sell all week.

'You told how Al Allen completely canvassed the same city block. He called on the same people and sold 66 new accident contracts. I remembered your statement, "It can't be done some may think, but—Al did it." I believed you. I was ready.

'I remembered the self-starter you gave us: *DO IT NOW!*

'I went to my card records and analysed ten "dead" accounts. I prepared what might previously have seemed to be an enormous program to present to each. I repeated the self-starter *DO IT NOW!* several times. And then I called on the ten accounts with a positive mental attitude and made eight large sales. It is amazing—truly amazing—what PMA will do for the salesmen who use its power!'

Now Edwin H. East was ready when he heard the talk on motivation. He listened to the message that was applicable to him. He was searching for something. And he found what he was looking for. Our purpose in relating this particular story is that you, too, have read about Al Allen. But you may not have seen how you could apply the principle to your own experience. Edwin H. East did. And you can, too.

Now, however, I want you to learn the self-starter, *DO IT NOW!*

Sometimes a decision to act immediately can make your wildest dreams come true. It worked that way for Manley Sweazey.

You can mix business and pleasure. Manley loved hunting and fishing. His idea of the good life was to hike fifty miles into the woods with his pole and his rifle, and hike back a couple of days later exhausted, muddy and very happy.

The only trouble with this hobby was that it took too much time out from his work as an insurance salesman. Then one day as he reluctantly left a favourite bass lake and headed back to his desk, Manley had a wild idea. Suppose, somewhere, there were people living in a wilderness—people who needed insurance. Then he could work and be out-of-doors at the same time! And indeed, Manley discovered, there was such a group of people: the men who worked for the Alaska Railroad. They lived in scattered section-houses strung out along the 500-mile length of the track. What if he were to sell insurance to these railroad men, and to the trappers and gold miners along the route?

The same day that the idea came to him, Sweazey began making positive plans. He consulted a travel agent and began packing. He didn't pause to let doubts creep in and frighten him into believing that his idea might be scatterbrained...that it might fail. Instead of picking the idea apart for its flaws, he took a boat to Seward, Alaska.

He walked the length of the railroad many, many times. 'Walking Sweazey', as he was called, became a welcome sight to these isolated families, not only because he sold insurance when no one else had thought them worth bothering with, but because he represented the outside world. He went the extra mile. For he taught himself how to cut hair and did it free of charge. He taught himself how to cook, too. Since the single men ate mostly canned foods and bacon, Manley, with his culinary skills, was a welcome guest. And all the while he was doing what came naturally. He was doing what he wanted to do: tramping the hills, hunting, fishing and— as he puts it, 'living the life of Sweazey!'

In the life insurance business there is a special place of honour reserved for men who sell over a million dollars' worth of business in one year. It is called the Million Dollar Round Table. Now the remarkable and almost unbelievable part of Manley Sweazey's story is that: having acted on his impulse, having taken off for the wilds of Alaska, having walked the railroad where no one else had bothered to go, he did his million dollars of business and more, in a single year, to take his place at the Round Table.

And none of it would have happened if he had hesitated to employ the secret of getting things done when his 'wild' idea came to him.

Memorize the self-starter *DO IT NOW!*

DO IT NOW! can affect every phase of your life. It can help you do the things you should do, but don't feel like doing. It can keep you from procrastinating when an unpleasant duty faces you. But it can also help you as it did Manley Sweazey, to do those things that you *want* to do. It helps you seize those precious moments which, if lost, may never be retrieved. The endearing word to a friend, for example. The telephone call to an associate, just telling him that you admire him. All in response to the self-starter: *DO IT NOW!*

Write yourself a letter. Here is an idea to help you get started. Sit down and write yourself a letter, telling the things you always intended to do as though they had already been accomplished—some personal, some charitable and other community projects. Write the letter as if a biographer were writing about the wonderful person you really are when you come under the influence of PMA. But don't stop there. Use the secret of getting things done. Respond to the self-starter *DO IT NOW!*

Remember, regardless of what you have been or what you are, you can be what you want to be if you *act* with PMA.

> **POINTS TO REMEMBER**
>
> 1. Develop habit through repetition.
> 2. The self-starter *DO IT NOW!* is an important self-motivator.
> 3. Application of the Mastermind alliance.

10

WILL YOU MASTER MONEY? OR WILL IT MASTER YOU?

Anything that robs you of peace of mind robs you of life's greatest wealth. You may lose peace of mind by pursuing money too anxiously, or by trying to acquire more money than you can spend wisely. Money you earn through constructive work is the money most likely to benefit you. It is a mistake to deprive young people of the need to know life through work. Anyone can save, and the effort you make toward saving a percentage of your income gives you a true knowledge of the value of money. Saving also prepares you to handle many opportunities which otherwise might slip by.

In my explorations of the points of view of young people I rarely find a great appreciation of money, most especially when a good sum of money is yet to be earned. This is proper enough. A lack of money makes the business of living so difficult it is very likely to destroy peace of mind.

So the young man pursues money. For a good part of his life he is likely to have no difficulty whatsoever in spending as much as he makes. If he has a family, they help him spend it. A successful man, however, is not very old before he begins to accumulate some money beyond his immediate needs and his household bank account. This money is likely to go into investments, real estate and the like.

Be he a truly positive-minded man, he will soon own considerable amounts of both property and money. And somewhere along the line he will have passed an invisible border. He is now rich in the sense that he has a considerable surplus above his needs. Undoubtedly he can fulfil any reasonable want. And so, while his financial records show he is rich, his inward and very private record should show he has peace of mind.

He will have peace of mind—if he has mastered money. He will not—if money has mastered him.

A man who makes a big splash may be a man who has gone overboard. The 'big splash' is the big show of one's material wealth. I have freely admitted my own weakness for making a big splash in the days of my Catskill estate which I was fortunate enough to lose before it permanently harmed me. Not every man is endangered by making a vast show of his wealth, and some seem to thrive on it. Others enter upon such conspicuous display that obviously they have gone overboard—their souls are drowning in their sea of dollars.

Some years ago a man who had earned several million dollars suddenly went bankrupt. When the lawyers searched his assets, they found a large warehouse filled with valuable antique furniture, magnificent paintings and the like. They all belonged to the man who was bankrupt and he had paid for them in cash. But had he ever enjoyed them? Most of those precious items never had been unpacked! He liked to talk about his treasures, however, and make himself sound like a veritable Croesus. Such an accumulation mania is at the opposite pole from a mind that knows peace.

'They are going to take it away from me!' The fear of poverty has a strange and ugly first cousin. It is the rich man's fear that his money will be taken away from him; or that he will not be allowed to pile up his money into ten times the sum he possibly could use—twenty times—thirty times!

I once knew a majority stockholder of the fabulous Coca-Cola Company. He had gathered money in many ways, and was worth about twenty-five million dollars. Did he have peace of mind? He had a mind filled with hatred and mistrust. His worst hatred was directed toward the government. Although he was then well in his eighties, he always prophesied that the government would cause him to die a pauper.

The last time I ever saw him, he asked me a most significant question, 'If you were in my place, what would you do to protect your peace of mind and save your money?'

I had determined that for the sake of my own peace of mind I never would start a quarrel with this man; but, if he ever asked me a direct question, he would receive a direct answer. Even so, I asked him now if he wanted my honest opinion. 'Yes!' he said. 'Naturally'

'Well,' said I, 'if I were in your place and wanted peace of mind I would not save my money. Your peace of mind and your money have become enemies who cannot live side by side. If I were you, I would first convert all my money into United States Savings Bonds so that it would go to work for the benefit of all the people. Then I would pile all those bonds into my fireplace and set fire to them. And as I watched my money go up the chimney, I would watch a great deal of my unhappiness burn away.'

My friend snapped, 'Don't be facetious!'

'I was never more serious in my life,' I replied. 'If I had your fortune and it deprived me of my peace of mind, I would first put my money where it would be well distributed and then I would burn every symbol of my government's debt to me. Then I would go to bed and sleep like a child and wake up feeling peaceful and free.'

I did not expect this man to follow my advice. To the day he died he lived in fear and bitterness, and I believe that the illness and debility which dogged him long before he died was rooted in his love—not of mankind, but of money.

PEACE OVER POWER

There are very few people for whom advice to burn their money would be good advice. The principle is what holds for every one of us. Nothing, absolutely nothing is as precious as your peace of mind. Few young people see this. Some people see it as they gain more experience. Many never see it. Remember, you can be rich with peace of mind, but if money or anything else gets in the way of your peace of mind, choose peace of mind and let the other go.

Notice I made no attempt to evaluate my friend's complaint against the government. His complaint may in some ways have been justified. It was his attitude I drove at—an attitude of fear and distrust while he was at least twenty-five times a millionaire and could have done so much toward making himself and others happy.

How much money does a man need? Andrew Carnegie certainly had a firm hold on methods for making money. In his later years, his earnest wish was to give this 'know-how' to the average man. Mr Carnegie was one of the first of the enlightened industrialists who saw how important it is for a nation to spread its wealth.

He saw that millions can be rich in the sense of having plenty. He also saw that, in the nature of things, the man who has millions always will be an exception. He saw that a goal of 'millions' of even 'a million' is not the right goal for the majority of men. For many, such a goal sets up strains which deny peace of mind. They may give up too much that is necessary for men of their personality, and so end with nothing. He admonished me again and again to make this clear, and I have done my best to do so.

How much money, then, does a man need?

As much as will keep him and his loved ones in what he considers solid comfort, along with enough luxury so that he may feel he has tasted the treats of life.

Aiming for this, and always maintaining his peace of mind, he conditions himself to a full use of his self-confident faith. And lo! out of this conditioning he often finds a moneymaking power beyond his dreams. For such a man, excess money never will be a curse. He knows how to live, so he knows how to broaden his life. He has never tried to cheat others, so he knows how to help others.

The man who wanted a hundred billion dollars. A student of mine once flew all the way from India to have an interview with me. First he sent me a letter in which he stated that his major purpose in life was to accumulate one hundred times as much wealth as Henry Ford had accumulated, or about one hundred billion dollars. He wished to be one hundred thousand times a millionaire.

When at length we sat in my study, I asked him what he would do with that modest little sum of money.

After some hesitation, he admitted, 'Honestly, I don't know.' 'Well,' I said, 'the possession of one hundred billion dollars by one individual poses a threat to the world. But let us put that aside. If you desired to spend the sum in helping the people of India overcome the superstitions and outmoded customs which have held them in bondage for centuries, I'd have some sympathy with you. It seems to me that you just want the money for the sake of outdoing Henry Ford.'

He thought awhile and admitted this was so. I helped him search himself, and he saw that in using the Science of Personal Achievement he had 'taken the bit in his teeth' and was galloping beyond control. What the mind builds in imagination, the mind can indeed build in reality; but we speak of a mind in good balance. Discussing his affairs, he came to see that a quarter of a million dollars would buy him what he really wanted. With that realization, the tense businessman—he was an importer—relaxed and said he felt much better.

This story's sequel involves another of those 'coincidences'.

I do not believe are really coincidences. Before this man returned to India I helped him secure several contracts for the sale of American-made products in his homeland. His profit eventually amounted to just a little over a quarter of a million dollars.

Money that benefits you most often comes from work that benefits you. I planted the idea that one can insure that his money and property go to persons of his choice when he dies. Unlike death itself, the bequeathing of assets is a controllable circumstance.

You are going to make money; and when you do, please be careful that such a bequest does not rob an inheritor of his peace of mind.

It has been said, and with reason, that a rich man's son often does not display the ability his father had. I believe that many rich men's sons are robbed of this ability because they inherit their fathers' money. By and large, the 'old man' worked for his money. His money came to him side by side with the development of his insight, his ability, his knowledge of people and his knowledge of the world. He was not given riches by his father; he was given riches by his work.

Now let us look at the son. All his life he has lived in the midst of money and the many comforts which money buys. He knows he is going to inherit great amounts of money. Assuming that he does have the inherent willingness to work hard—what happens to that willingness? In many cases it is replaced by a willingness to get something for nothing, and thus he never learns one of the basic lessons of life.

Great fortunes or modest fortunes are a blessing only when they are used in good part to benefit others. No father benefits his son when he robs him of initiative. No testator favours a beneficiary by making it unnecessary for him to work. You may wish to shield your inheritors from the meanness of poverty. Well and good! Beyond that, do not shield them from life with a wall of money. Let them have the priceless opportunity of building better lives with their own life-taught wisdom and their own constructive work.

In my youth, I worked as a secretary to a wealthy lawyer who had two sons somewhat older than myself. These youths attended the University of Virginia. It became my duty to make up for each of them a monthly check for one hundred dollars as spending money. In those days a hundred dollars would buy three or four times what it will today. How I envied those boys!

When I had been in business college, learning how to earn my own living, I had often gone hungry because I literally did not have a cent in my pocket. I vividly recall standing in front of a store and longing for some apples which were priced six for a dime. At length I went in and sold the storekeeper on the idea of trusting me for the dime until I got through school and began to earn money. Such were my memories as I made out those magnificent monthly checks.

By and by my employer's sons came home with their

diplomas. They also came home conditioned to easy living and with little idea of what work is all about. Were they inherently as capable as their father? We shall never know. One of them was put into a good job in a bank his father owned, and another was made manager of one of his father's coal mines.

Ten years later they had completely wrecked their father' s fortune and his health as well.

I no longer envy anyone, for envy is no part of peace of mind. As I look back, I am grateful that I had to undergo such experiences as negotiating a ten-cent long-term credit. And I am grateful that, when I began to earn money, my earning power became part of my self-fulfilment. I am even glad that when I made mistakes and lost money, I had no rich father to see me through, for I found a mighty teacher in adversity.

My book *Think and Grow Rich* has been read by perhaps seven million men and women. In the twenty years since it was published I have been able to talk to some of these people, and I see that some have used the book to help them become truly rich. But some have used it to help them become rich in money only.

THE TWELVE GREAT RICHES OF LIFE:

1. l. A positive mental attitude
2. Sound physical health
3. Harmony in human relationships
4. Freedom from all forms of fear
5. The hope of future achievement
6. The capacity for faith
7. A willingness to share one's blessings
8. A labour of love as an occupation
9. An open mind on all subjects

10. Self-discipline in all circumstances
11. The capacity to understand others
12. Sufficient money

These are the riches which can and should go along with peace of mind. Notice I have set money in the last place, and this despite my insisting that it is very difficult to have peace of mind without sufficient money. I set it there because you yourself will automatically give emphasis to money. Now and then, therefore, I must remind you to de-emphasize it and remember this: money will buy a great deal but it will not buy peace of mind—it only will help you find peace of mind. But neither money nor anything else can help you find peace of mind unless you begin the journey from within yourself.

Basic steps in building your income. I have been told that it is not good logic to warn people of the dangers of misusing money, when probably they do not have enough money to make them worry about misusing it. I would follow this advice if I were writing a book merely about how to earn money. This book also is concerned with showing you where you are going and how the world looks when you get there. It helps you build correct attitudes right at the start.

As long as we have pointed firmly at those attitudes, however—as we shall point again—I shall set down some practical ways in which a person who has little or no capital can begin to build his wealth. Each of these ways is specific unto itself, so to speak, but is capable of almost infinite modification. It is up to you to pause as you read and apply these procedures to yourself, your talents, your surroundings and, above all, your goals.

1. Get other people to help their own businesses by helping yours. A young life insurance salesman was having trouble in placing policies with heads of families. Using this adversity as a springboard, he wondered why he could not sell insurance to the very same men, not in their role as heads of families but in their role as businessmen. After all, money taken out of the family budget is money gone; but a business expense offers an opportunity of bringing back the expended sum many times over.

He began with a leading restaurant owner in his town. He pointed out to this man that he might very well advertise that the food he served was so wholesome and sustaining that people who ate in his restaurant were likely to live longer. The restaurateur said this was indeed so and he intended to make sure it always was so. Good, said the insurance man, and explained the rest of the plan. The restaurateur was to offer to insure the life of each regular customer for one thousand dollars. Details were worked out and the offer made the restaurant's business boom. Needless to say, it helped the young insurance man.

He extended the idea to a group of filling stations, to a large grocery and to others. I am not positive it was this man who originated the idea of adding life insurance to mortgages so that the mortgage would be paid off if the purchaser died—but he certainly made good use of this angle as well.

Now stop and think: how can you get other people to help their own businesses by helping yours?

2. Show someone how he can get more for his money. Here we are not talking about setting yourself up as a business adviser, so that people seek you out to learn how they can get more for their money. We assume that the initiative must be yours.

Here is how one man did it:

Working at a low salary for a distributor of magazines, he took notice of many different kinds of printing. As with another man I have mentioned in this book, he noticed that many of the printing jobs could have been done with more taste and style.

Now, this young chap was discovering that most jobs of any kind are not done as well as they could be. Take note of this, for a fortune can be made on the idea.

The young man found out more about printing, then went to a large printing firm. He arranged to bring in printing jobs at a 10 per cent commission. He then went to large users of printed matter and collected a great many samples, which he took home and studied.

Selecting two or three brochures which obviously needed improvement, he arranged with a free-lance commercial artist to prepare a sample layout for each, on the promise of a fair fee if the job went through. An advertising copywriter who had spare time contributed his own talents on the same basis. Armed now with a good 'rough' of an improved job, the young man took the brochures to the firms which had issued them and simply showed how much better they could be.

Now, let us look into some of the practical psychology at work here.

To begin with, a person or a company may go on almost forever with some condition or process or product that 'gets by'. He may not realize he is merely getting by; or if he does, he is too busy or too lazy to do anything about it.

Along comes someone who makes him dissatisfied with what he has and in the same moment shows him how to do better. Moreover, the work is all done for him. Why not take advantage of it?

Now stop and think: how can you show someone how he can get more for his money? Extend that: how can you help someone get more for his money in such a way that he will thereafter depend on you to show him again and again?

3. Bring producer and consumer together. The farmer used to have a tough time bringing his goods to market. Imagine an isolated farm in hilly country, on a road that was mostly mud, and with horse and wagon the only means of transportation. Still, the farmer had to bring his produce to town and so he did by hook or by crook.

Everything in our economy intermeshes with everything else. As the automobile came in, roads had to be improved and they were. Now the farmer could carry his goods five to ten times the distance he used to and still get home the same night. Soon someone found he could set up marketing centres between towns, and draw on the increasing car traffic for customers while the farmers were very glad to be a continued source of supply.

Farmers used to depend on peddlers who came by perhaps twice a year, sometimes on foot with huge packs on their backs. Unrolling his pack on the kitchen table, the peddler would provide the farmer's wife with needles and the like, the farmer with tobacco and fish hooks—and above all, with news. How hungry people used to be for news! The peddlers invariably had more money than the farmers, for they performed the valuable function of bringing producer and consumer together.

When the farmer wanted to sell or buy a horse, he often was assisted by a broker who helped both parties reach an agreement on price, then sealed the bargain by making them shake hands. The broker, too, generally made more money than the farmers because he brought producer and consumer together.

Recently I read of complaints by shoppers in the Soviet Union. It seems they spend endless hours standing on line in front of separate, specialized food stores. Eventually they may adopt the American idea of bringing many producers and many consumers together in convenient supermarkets.

Fortunes have been made in this revolution in merchandising, especially as supermarkets—and their sprawling parking lots—have moved into the suburbs and even far out into the country. Fringe benefits have come to many property owners who saw how to ride along with the trend.

A woman lived alone on twenty poor acres which had mostly been taken over by scrub pine. At last she decided to sell the old homestead. Neighbours told her, sighing, that she would never get much for it. A local real estate man made her a pitiable offer.

This woman, however, was one of those elderly (in years) people who never had seen any reason why her mind should not remain alert. She told herself that her farm must be good for something. She decided to spend thirty days in an intensive investigation of what run-down farms are good for. Before the end of that thirty days she had found she could sell it as a base for a riding stable, complete with pasture and pleasant riding trails, for twice what the real estate man had offered.

But also she had studied several supermarkets in the area and had concluded that her farm would make a good supermarket site. She sold out finally to a supermarket for five times what the real estate man had offered.

When roads were paved and transportation by automobile became so easy, it was predicted that the mail-order house would disappear. After all, why should a person buy from a catalogue when he can buy from the store itself? Such firms as Sears, Roebuck and Montgomery Ward nevertheless continue to flourish.

Despite constant rises in postage rates, thousands of mail-order businesses thrive on selling everything from postage scales with the new rates printed on them, to books, household furnishings, preserved and fresh food, vitamins, equipment for hobbies, boat supplies… the list is almost endless.

Why is this so? Because times may change but universal needs always continue. Showing a person that he can write his name and address on an order form and drop it into the mail, and be assured of prompt delivery of something he wants, continues to be a good way to bring producer and consumer together.

Sometimes the producer sells directly to the consumer. Far more often the consumer buys from a middle man who assumes retail selling as his special function or from a manufacturer's representative.

Now stop and think: how can you bring producer and consumer together?

Some of the money you earn should stay with you. Certainly we have not exhausted the subject of making money! You may even feel that in giving the subject a once-over lightly treatment, I have not done justice to it. I suggest, however, that you reread the foregoing three items and see in how many ways you can relate yourself to them. They have a great universality. Stretch them—you need not be too literal—and you will find they cover a vast variety of business situations, a broad horizon of opportunities. Note that they have not been tied to any particular craft or skill, since the fields mentioned are illustrative of many others.

You will find it an interesting exercise to see how many incidents of your own affairs can be fitted into one or more of those three categories. If you will put aside your own work and see yourself as a consumer, you certainly will 'fit'! We shall touch upon many other principles which help hard-working men make money.

We still are talking about money and peace of mind.

Nobody who goes too deeply into debt can count on having

peace of mind. You may have it for a time, but now and again the debt comes into your consciousness and you feel you are not quite your own master; somebody else owns a piece of you. I am not talking here of ordinary business credit without which business hardly could exist, but more of personal debts.

Having some money laid away is a means of avoiding the uncertainty and often the embarrassment that goes with incurring a personal debt. But saving does more for you than merely make it possible to spend the money you save. Saving gives you the habit of gauging your money against your needs. It helps to remind you that money is good only because of what it can buy in goods and services, and again it helps you gauge what you need in the way of goods and services.

POINTS TO REMEMBER

1. Peace of mind is life's greatest wealth.
2. Money that benefits you most often comes from work that benefits you.
3. Never-ending greed for money will lead to your downfall.

11

GROWTH THROUGH STRUGGLE

The necessity for struggle is one of the clever devices through which nature *forces* individuals to expand, develop, progress and become strong through resistance. Struggle can, and does, become either an ordeal or a magnificent experience through which the individual expresses gratitude for the opportunity to conquer the cause of his struggle.

Life, from birth until death, is literally an unbroken record of an ever-increasing variety of struggles, which no individual can avoid.

Mastery of ignorance calls for struggle. Education involves eternal struggle, and every day is commencement day because education is cumulative. It is a lifetime job.

The accumulation of material riches abounds in the necessity for struggle; so much so in fact that many individuals actually kill themselves early in life due to anxiety and overexertion in the effort to acquire more money than they need.

Maintenance of sound physical health calls for eternal struggle with the multifarious enemies of sound health: struggle for food and shelter; struggle for an opportunity to earn a living; struggle to hold a job; struggle to gain recognition in a profession; struggle to keep a business out of bankruptcy.

Look in whatever direction we may, and we find that there

is hardly a circumstance of daily life which does not call for individual struggle in order to survive.

We are forced to recognize that this great universal necessity for struggle must have a definite and useful purpose. That purpose is to force the individual to sharpen his wits, arouse his enthusiasm, build up his spirit of Faith, gain definiteness of purpose, develop his power of will, inspire his faculty of imagination to give him new uses for old ideas and concepts and *thereby fulfil some unknown mission for which he may have been born.*

Struggle keeps man from going to sleep with self-satisfaction or laziness, and forces him onward and upward in the fulfilment of his mission in life, and he thereby makes his individual contribution to whatever may be the Universal Purpose of mankind on earth.

Strength, both physical and spiritual, is the product of struggle!

'Do the thing,' said Emerson, 'and you shall have the power.'

Meet struggle and master it, says nature, and you shall have *strength and wisdom sufficient for all your needs.*

If you wish a strong arm, says nature, give it systematic use under the weight of a three-pound hammer and soon you will have muscles like bands of steel. If you do not wish a strong arm, says nature, tie it in a sling, take it out of use and remove the cause for struggle, and its strength will wither and die.

In every form of life, atrophy and death come from idleness! The only thing nature will not tolerate is idleness. Through the necessity for struggle and the Law of Change nature keeps everything throughout the universe in a constant state of ux. Nothing, from the electrons and the protons of matter to the suns and planets which oat throughout space, is ever still for a single second. Nature's motto is: keep moving or perish! There is no halfway ground, no compromise, no exceptions for any reason whatsoever.

And should you doubt that nature intends every individual to keep struggling or perish, observe what takes place with the person who makes his fortune and 'retires'—gives up the struggle because he no longer believes it is necessary.

PRINCIPLE OF COSMIC HABIT FORCE

The strongest trees are not those in heavily protected forests, but the trees which stand in open spaces where they are in constant struggle with wind and all the elements of weather.

My grandfather was a wagon maker. In clearing his land for the production of crops, he always left a few oaks standing in the open elds, where they could be toughened by exposure. These he later cut and used for the 'fellows' needed in making wagon wheels— timber that could be bent into arc-shaped segments without breaking in the process. He found that trees protected by the forest could not produce the sort of timber he required. It was too soft and brittle because it had not been under the necessity for struggle—the self-same reason why some people are 'soft' and unprepared to cope with the resistances of life.

Most people go through life by the line of least resistance in every circumstance where they can make a choice. They do not recognize *that following the line of least resistance makes all rivers, and some men, crooked!*

There may be some pain in most forms of struggle, but nature compensates the individual for the pain in the form of *power and strength and wisdom which come from practical experience.*

While organizing the Science of Success philosophy, I made the revealing discovery that all the more successful leaders, in every calling, in every profession, and every walk of life, had gained their leadership in almost exact ratio to the extent of their struggles in the attainment of their leadership.

I observed, with profound interest, that no man who had not been thoroughly tested by the necessity of struggle, seemed ever to have been chosen as a leader in times of great crises during the interim between the stone age and our present day civilization.

Careful study of the entire record of civilization itself, from the age of the cave man to the present, shows clearly that it is the product of eternal struggle. Yes, struggle definitely is one of the Creator's devices for forcing individuals to respond to the Law of Change in order that the overall plan of the universe may be carried out.

When any individual reconciles himself to the state of mind wherein he is willing to accept largess from the government, instead of supplying his needs through personal initiative, that individual is on the road to decay and spiritual blindness. When a majority of the people of any nation give up their inherited prerogative right to make their own way through struggle, *history shows clearly that the entire nation is in a tailspin of decay that inevitably must end in extinction.*

The individual who not only is willing to live on the public treasury, *but demands that he be fed from it,* is already dead spiritually. The physical body still walks, but it is only an empty shell whose only hope for the future is a funeral. This, of course, has reference only to able-bodied people who quit the struggle because they are too indifferent or too lazy to keep on growing through the Law of Change and the urge for struggle.

For twenty odd years I was forced to struggle in mastering the problems incidental to my work in organizing the world's first practical philosophy of success. First, I was forced to struggle in preparing myself with the necessary knowledge to produce the philosophy. Secondly, I was forced to struggle to maintain myself economically while doing the research necessary to organize the philosophy. Then I met with still greater necessity for struggle while gaining recognition from the world for myself and the philosophy.

Twenty years of struggle without any direct financial compensation is an experience not calculated to give one sustained hope, but it was the price I had to pay for a philosophy which was destined to bene t untold numbers of people, many of whom were not born when I began my work.

Discouraging? Heartbreaking? Not at all, for I recognized from the beginning that out of my struggle would come triumph and victory in proportion to the labours invested in my task. In this hope I have not been disappointed, but I have been overwhelmed with the bountiful manner in which the world has responded and paid me tribute for the long years of struggle that went into my work.

Also, I have gained from my struggle something of still greater and more profound value. It is recognition that through my struggles I *have reached deeply into the spiritual wells of my soul*, and there I have found powers available for every purpose I may desire —powers I never knew I possessed, *and never would have discovered except by the means of struggle!*

Through my struggles I discovered, and learned how to make use of, the magical Eight Princes of Guidance described in a previous chapter—the unseen friends who administer to all of my physical, financial and spiritual needs, who work for me while I sleep and while I am awake.

Also, it was through my struggles that the great Law of Cosmic Habitforce (the law that is the fixer of all habits, the comptroller of all natural laws) was revealed to me; the law which led me, at long last, to where I was ready to give the world the bene t of my experiences through struggle.

From my experiences with struggle I discovered that the Creator never singles out an individual for an important service to mankind without first testing him, through struggle, in proportion to the nature of the service he is to render. Thus, through struggle, I learned to interpret the laws, purposes and working plans of the Creator as they related to me and to mankind in general.

What greater benefits could anyone desire from struggle?

What greater rewards could anyone gain from any other cause?

Briefly we have reviewed only four of Life's Miracles, but these are by no means the more important of the miracles we are to inspect on our trip through Nature's Wonderland Valley.

However, we have witnessed enough on our trip to convince us that there is good in all circumstances which touch or influence our lives, whether they be circumstances over which we have complete control or those over which we have no control *except the control of our mental reaction to them.*

As we proceed on our trip, through the chapters to follow, our minds should unfold until we recognize that circumstances which we may regard as unpleasant may be a part of the Creator's overall plan in connection with human destiny on this earth. The major purpose of this chapter is to broaden the mind so it may encompass and envision important facts of life *outside of those which immediately concern* the individual.

Peace of mind is not possible without this capacity for panoramic vision of the entire picture and purpose of life. We must recognize that our individual incarnation, through which we are tossed into this material world without ceremony and without our consent, was for a purpose above and beyond our individual pleasures and desires.

Once we understand this broader purpose of life we become reconciled to the experiences of struggle we must undergo while passing this way, and we accept them as circumstances of opportunity through which we may prepare ourselves for still higher and better planes of existence than the one on which we now dwell.

POINTS TO REMEMBER

1. Struggle is a necessity to become stronger.
2. Struggle makes you contribute to whatever may be your Universal Purpose on earth.
3. Keep moving or perish!

www.ingramcontent.com/pod-product-compliance
Lightning Source LLC
Chambersburg PA
CBHW032230080426
42735CB00008B/790